# I TALKED WITH HIM THIS MORNING

## A Collection of Devotional Poems
From Morning Prayer

By C. R. Hill, Jr.

Copyright 2014 by C.R. Hill, Jr.

I Talked With Him This Morning
Published by Yawn's Publishing
198 North Street
Canton, GA 30114
www.yawnspublishing.com

Library of Congress Control Number: 2015937152

ISBN: 978-1-940395-91-3   paperback
978-1-940395-92-0    eBook

Printed in the United States

# Introduction

*I Talked With Him This Morning* is a collection of poems that have arisen out of my morning meditation over the past three and a half years since retiring. The collection began as a continuation of my custom of writing a poem each week that would capture the main point of the sermon I was preaching the upcoming Sunday. It was my intention that by capturing the main point of the sermon in a brief poem and having that printed on the bulletin each week, members of the congregation could take it home and think about it during the week. Having it in something of rhyming verse made it easier to remember and chew on.

One of the things I enjoyed the most about my pastoral ministry was the preaching and the discipline of sermon preparation. To my surprise the thing I missed the most when I retired was the discipline of preparing those messages. I must confess that for a few months after retiring I found myself floundering for lack of the spiritual discipline that the need to prepare a sermon each week had demanded. At first I thought that I would supplement that discipline by writing a devotional blog. However, writing a brief devotional message and preparing an entire sermon are different things and I discovered very quickly that there was a whole host of writers including my own daughter, April Hawkins, that were much better at it than myself. I felt that I really had nothing unique to add to the body of material that was already out there.

Meanwhile another discipline that I had begun during my time as pastor of Canton First United Methodist Church was a pattern for daily prayer and meditation that I called "Powder House Prayers". Fairly early on after retiring I had taken that pattern and combined it with the pattern I had used in my sermon preparation. Using a guide for daily scripture reading I address the scripture of the day in the same manner that I had done in preparing sermons, as a conversation between myself and God. In this way I was seeking to discern the central message the passage had for me in that moment. I would then seek out the specific verse that spoke the clearest in that conversation and conclude by asking God for a poem to capture the essence of the message of that day.

It is from these conversations with God through the scriptures that these poems have come. Sometime later I realized that through these poems I did have something unique to add to the conversation of devotional blogs, and I began posting them. Most often I posted them very quickly after writing them, always without a second set of eyes to proofread them, and usually without allowing enough time for them to "cool" so that I might catch mistakes in spelling etc., or tweak a line here and there to make the meaning clearer, or the line flow more smoothly. As these poems are now offered here that editing process has taken place.

As for the scripture readings that accompany each poem they are all from the *King James Version* of the *Bible.* The language of the *King James* is beautiful and because it is so different from the way we now speak it tends to lend itself more easily to memorization. However, I encourage the reader to also read these passages from a more recent translation of the scriptures. And read the verses cited here in the larger context of the chapter in which they occur. Engage them in conversation thereby letting God's message for your life emerge, and may God bless you through the process.

Dedicated To the Glory of God The Father
And to The Son Jesus Christ The Lord and Savior of All
Creation
And to The Holy Spirit Who Inspires God's Word In Us

And in Honor of My Wife
Jacqueline W. Hill
Whose Love and Support for Over Fifty Years
Has Blessed Me Beyond Measure

# Acknowledgements

I must gratefully acknowledge the innumerable army of family members, mentors, teachers, parishioners, colleagues, assistants, patients, coworkers, friends, and even strangers whose lives, by the mercy and grace of God in Jesus Christ, have composed the soil in which I have been rooted, and from which I have grown.  Without that innumerable army of people none of who I am or what I have done here or elsewhere would exist.

## Thank You

# Contents

C.R. Hill, Jr.

# A Candle Lit

A candle lit in a corner dark,
May seem a meager thing,
Yet the light given by its flame,
Can a soul from darkness bring.

And while a single candle is small,
When others by it catch fire,
The light they give to all around,
Can the heart of the world inspire.

O let me be such a single light,
In my corner of this world,
And may another life light up,
'Til we the light of God unfurl.

Then may the world look on,
To see the path of holy ways,
And from its present darkened path,
Turn to the path of heavenly praise.

———————

"Neither do men light a candle,
And put it under a bushel, but on a candlestick;
and it giveth light unto all that are in the house."
Matthew 5:15 KJV

## A Chosen Race

Before one can ever a follower be,
Of Jesus Christ the Lord,
Before one can ever be used,
They are called by God's own Word.

The decision that one makes to follow,
Is not first the choice of one's will;
It is the will's response to God,
Who with his Spirit does one fill.

There is the freedom that one has,
To refuse God's Spirit's call,
Then try to follow one's own path,
But in the end that one will fall.

Chosen vessels Christ's followers are,
Disciples sent the lost to win,
As ambassadors of salvation's news,
Of God's reconciling the world to him.

———————

"Ye have not chosen me, but I have chosen you,
and ordained you, that ye should go and bring forth fruit,
and *that* your fruit should remain: that whatsoever
ye shall ask of the Father in my name, he may give it you."
John 15: 16 KJV

"But ye are a chosen generation, a royal priesthood,
a holy nation, a peculiar people; that ye should show forth the praises
of him who hath called you out of darkness into his marvelous light."
1Peter 2: 9 KJV

C.R. Hill, Jr.

## A Climber's Heart

Like a hiker on that mountain trail,
I carry a heavy pack.
Too many things I think I need,
To load upon my back.

I struggle over the rocky climbs,
With every muscle strained,
Too exhausted when I top the ridge,
To even see the view I've gained.

Like that hiker with the heavy pack,
So my heart is packed too full,
I cannot gain the heights of God,
With a heart of things that downward pull.

Help me, Lord, to choose the things,
That I pack within my heart,
That will strengthen me for the climb,
And not from your pathway part.

———

"And when they had brought their ships to land,
they forsook all, and followed him."
Luke 5: 11 KJV

## A Gift with All To Share

A gift God has placed into my hands,
With which I am to trade,
So that others my also receive,
The gift for them he made.

This gift, the news that in Jesus Christ,
He is all human sin forgiving,
And in his love and grace,
He desires people always to be living.

Yet we who have this gift received,
Too often keep it hidden,
We fear that if we make it known,
It will be stolen or forbidden.

Not so! Not so!
It has been given to be shared!
Go tell the news to all you see,
And for his coming be prepared!

---

"For unto every one that hath shall be given,
and he shall have abundance:
but from him that hath not shall be taken away
even that which he hath."
Matthew 25:29 KJV

# A Heart Divided

Like the rich young ruler I find myself,
Unwilling to yield full surrender.
I cling to the relics of my fleeting treasures,
While to God refusing devotion to render.

It is not a problem I have all alone,
It is the way that most of us live.
We spend all our time looking for that,
Which meaning for our living will give.

The problem - we seek that in the now,
In the things that the flesh can enjoy;
Only to find at the end of the day,
They are all things that death will destroy.

While the creator of life beckons and calls,
Saying, "Lose your life and find it in me.
I am the way the truth and the life,
Follow - and from death you will be free."

———————

"Wherefore do ye spend money for that which is not bread?
and your labour for that which satisfieth not?
hearken diligently unto me, and eat ye that which is good,
and let your soul delight itself in fatness."
Isaiah 55: 2 KJV

## A Mind Set Matter

"Set your mind on me,"
Is what I hear God say,
Yet I get so distracted,
By all the issues of the day.

The chores, the bills, fun things too,
All clamor for my attention.
Until my mind becomes so cluttered,
That I fail even God to mention.

Still he patiently watches and waits,
Until I crash into the wall,
Where in frustration and defeat,
I finally upon his name will call.

"I told you so," he never says,
For he knows I know that all too well.
Instead in grace he has me focus on,
What his word has to me to tell.

––––––––––

"For they that are after the flesh
do mind the things of the flesh;
but they that are after the Spirit
the things of the Spirit."
Romans 8:5 KJV,

C.R. Hill, Jr.

## A Prayer for Stillness

I usually set out to take on the day,
Relying for the most part on me.
I have a plan for what I want to do,
And too often fail God's plan to see.

I've too little time to pause by the way,
So I can consult with my Father's will.
I am in a big hurry to get on with things,
No time left over to just be still.

Yet the truth of it is I've no time at all,
For all of my time is in God's hands,
The only things that will last in the end,
Are those that conform to his plans.

So teach me O Lord, and help me to learn,
To take time each day to meet you.
Help me listen, and to then understand,
So I can then do what you want me to.

———

"Abide in me, and I in you.
As the branch cannot bear fruit of itself,
except it abide in the vine; no more can ye,
except ye abide in me."
John 15:4 KJV

## A Prescription for Daily Peace

We wake up every morning,
Wondering what the day has in store,
Will we have the things we need,
Of course we are always wanting more.

But none of us can see ahead,
Or know just what the day might hold.
God alone knows what the day will bring,
Or just how each hour will unfold.

So why not start out by trusting him?
Begin by seeking first his will.
For all the things we need for that,
God does from his abundance fill.

So be not anxious when you set out,
Upon your day each morn,
God already knows what you will need,
Before your day begins to dawn.

———

"And he said unto his disciples,
Therefore I say unto you,
Take no thought for your life,
what ye shall eat; neither for the body,
what ye shall put on. 23 The life is more
than meat, and the body *is more* than raiment.
31 But rather seek ye the kingdom of God;
And all these things shall be added unto you."
Luke 12: 22-23 & 31 KJV

C.R. Hill, Jr.

# A Race You Can't Lose

I was trying to run with weights on my feet,
It was like trying to run in iron shoes.
But when I put on the Gospel of Peace,
I could run like the wind with good news.

Too many times Jesus calls us to come,
To follow in faith where he leads,
But when we look around and don't focus on him,
We are like running in mud to our knees.

"Focus!" he shouts. "Keep your eyes fixed on me!"
Is the loud invitation he gives,
And the one among us who listens and does,
Is the one among us who lives.

"Remove those shoes that have you weighed down!
Put on instead the shoes of Good News!
Then take to the trail with me in the lead,
And you'll be running a race you can't lose."

———————

"How beautiful upon the mountains
are the feet of him that bringeth good tidings,
that publisheth peace; that bringeth good tidings
of good, that publisheth salvation;
that saith unto Zion, Thy God reigneth."
Isaiah 52: 7 KJV

I Talked With Him This Morning

## All Darkness Overcome

There are days when I am wowed,
By the wonder of God's Word.
Days when there comes so clear,
The greatest news I've heard.

I walk and work among folks each day,
Who in life are struggling so,
So many trials and troubles they have,
They are overcome by all life's woes.

Yet in the midst of all the trials,
There is God's news of life and hope.
They can place their hand in Jesus' palm,
And not in the darkness grope.

For in Jesus there is such light and life,
That it overcomes our darkest night.
He breathes a hope into our soul,
That secures our future bright!

––––––––

"Jesus saith unto her,
I am the resurrection, and the life;
he that believeth in me, though he were dead,
yet shall he live; 26 And whosoever liveth
and believeth in me shall never die.
Believest thou this?"
John 11: 25 & 26 KJV

Read John 10:31-11:44 &
1Corinthians 15:50-58

C.R. Hill, Jr.

## All to Grace I Owe

When I pause to reflect,
On how far I've come along my way,
It is all to God I owe the thanks,
For where I am today.

O as his grace has safely brought,
Me to this place I am,
I know that he will faithful be,
To finish in me his plan.

So I'll keep my trust in him,
For unknown days ahead,
I know through either storm or sun,
I have nothing to fear or dread.

When at last I reach the goal,
Of his wondrous promised land,
I know that Jesus will plea for me,
As before God's judgment bar I stand.

———————

Read Deuteronomy 6: 4 - 25

"Wherefore remember, that ye being in time past
Gentiles in the flesh, who are called Uncircumcision
by that which is called the Circumcision in the flesh made by hands;
12 That at that time ye were without Christ, being aliens
from the commonwealth of Israel, and strangers from
the covenants of promise, having no hope, and without God
in the world: 13 But now in Christ Jesus ye who sometimes
were far off are made nigh by the blood of Christ.."
Ephesians 2: 11 – 13 KJV

I Talked With Him This Morning

## Amid the Oaks Where Grace Abounds

In a little town beneath silent oaks,
There is to this day a quiet place,
Where once upon an April day,
A sinner found life-changing grace.

Down from God the grace did stream,
To embrace that sin-sick soul,
Then fill that lost and aimless life,
With the vision of God's goal.

Grace so precious from heaven sent,
Was then by a congregation shown,
As they embraced a sinner changed,
Before the fruits of change had grown.

Though the years and seasons change,
That grace continues to be extended,
Transforming lives because in this place,
A sinner was by Christ befriended.

————

"There is therefore now no condemnation
to them which are in Christ Jesus, who walk
not after the flesh, but after the Spirit.  2 For the law
of the Spirit of life in Christ Jesus hath made me
free from the law of sin and death."
Romans 8: 1 & 2 KJV

C.R. Hill, Jr.

## An Eternal Future Bright

There is a vision that fills my mind
Of God's eternal future bright.
A place where evil can not enter in,
Nor death shut out the light.

This the promise secured by Christ,
When upon the cross he died for sin,
Then rose again on Easter Day,
Life eternal for us to win.

Friend, look not to stocks and bonds,
Nor to arms and tools of force,
To make for you a secure hope;
In the end these make things worse.

But set your hope on Jesus Christ,
And in his great salvation trust.
An eternal home he has secured for us,
When we give up these robes of dust.

————

Read John 10:31—11:44 &
1Corinthians 15:50--58

"Behold, I shew you a mystery;
We shall not all sleep, but we shall all
be changed, 52 In a moment, in the
twinkling of an eye, at the last trump:
for the trumpet shall sound, and the dead
shall be raised incorruptible, and we shall
be changed. 53 For this corruptible must
put on incorruption, and this mortal
must put on immortality."
1Corinthians 15: 51-53 KJV

13

I Talked With Him This Morning

## O Bread That Feeds the Soul

God has sent to us his Bread of Life
In his precious Son our Lord.
His word – the food for which we long,
Also a sharpened two-edged sword.

For us the precious Son of God,
Has come to earth our souls to save,
To break the bonds of sin and death,
And overcome the grave.

We work and toil from dawn to dark,
Yet, our hearts do hunger still,
While those who eat the bread he gives,
Find he does their deepest hunger fill.

This is the promise he has given,
And his word cannot be broken,
"Come you hungry; eat the bread I give,
In every word that I have spoken."

———————

"Wherefore do ye spend money for that which is not bread?
and your labor for that which satisfieth not?
hearken diligently unto me, and eat ye that which is good,
and let your soul delight itself in fatness."
Isaiah 55: 2 KJV

"And Jesus said unto them, I am
the bread of life: he that cometh to me
shall never hunger; and he that believeth
on me shall never thirst."
John 6: 35 KJV

C.R. Hill, Jr.

# Arise, My Priest!

Blow the trumpet! Sound the charge!
Arouse the people of our God!
Put on the gospel armor,
Then march where Christ did trod.

For night has gripped the sons of earth,
Her daughters grope as blind.
Evil has their souls enslaved,
Capturing both their heart and mind.

But you, O sons and daughters,
Who are set free by God's great light,
Have the power to defeat the foe,
And shatter all the chains of night.

Rouse yourselves! Let shine your light!
Which is the Gospel that you bear,
Fear not to in the battle engage,
For the Lord our God is with you there.

———

"Therefore if any man be in Christ,
he is a new creature: old things are passed away;
behold, all things are become new.  18 And all things
are of God, who hath reconciled us to himself
by Jesus Christ, and hath given to us the ministry
of reconciliation;  19 To wit, that God was in Christ,
reconciling the world unto himself, not imputing their
trespasses unto them; and hath committed unto us
the word of reconciliation."
2Corinthians 5:17-19 KJV

## As Empty As a Child

I set out today with my head held in the air,
And with a swagger in my stride.
Of myself I was thinking really very well,
Confident in the reasons for my pride.

But then with Jesus I had my morning talk,
He promptly set me down as he explained,
That for boasting I had no reason to at all,
Nor could anything by it be gained.

"Humble yourself!" he said to me,
"Lean entirely upon my grace.
When you boast of what you've done,
You are not looking into my face."

I had to turn and look into his eyes,
Then all swagger and all pride did melt away.
Humbly I stared at his nail-pierced hands,
As I became as empty as a child today.

––––––––––

"At the same time came the disciples unto Jesus,
saying, Who is the greatest in the kingdom of heaven?
2 And Jesus called a little child unto him, and set him
in the midst of them, 3 And said, Verily I say unto you,
Except ye be converted, and become as little children,
ye shall not enter into the kingdom of heaven. 4 Whosoever
therefore shall humble himself as this little child, the same
is the greatest in the kingdom of heaven."
Matthew 18: 1-4 KJV

C.R. Hill, Jr.

## As Time Goes By

Days they come and days they go,
As time goes flying by.
Days begin to all look alike,
Til their purpose we deny.

But days are not for wasting time,
Each one –a treasured gift.
In each we are to seek God's face,
And his praises to uplift.

In each we are to do God's will,
And his kingdom's glory seek,
And listen for his still small voice,
As he to our heart does speak.

There in that special space of time,
Bounded by rising and setting sun,
We are to fill the time with news,
Of God's great salvation won.

---

"But seek ye first the kingdom of God,
and his righteousness; and all these things
shall be added unto you."
Matthew 6:33 KJV

## Ask To Receive

So many things we worry about,
And know not how to solve.
So many times we fret and stew,
Over something only God can resolve.

Yet we forget to take it to God,
Or follow the instructions he gives.
He says ask to receive if only you will,
For in so doing the seeker lives.

There is a hymn we sing in church,
That tells of God's promise so true,
"Only trust him, only trust him...."
And he will clear the path for you.

So when you are worrying, all in a stew,
Ask Jesus to help – turn it over to him,
See then what his grace can achieve,
And a victory you over all worry will win.

————

"Ask, and it shall be given you; seek, and
ye shall find; knock, and it shall be opened
unto you: 8 For every one that asketh
receiveth; and he that seeketh findeth;
and to him that knocketh it shall be opened."
Matthew 7: 7 & 8 KJV

"Ye lust, and have not; ye kill, and desire to have,
and cannot obtain: ye fight and war, yet ye have not,
because ye ask not. 3 Ye ask, and receive not,
because ye ask amiss, that ye may
consume it upon your lusts."
James 4: 2 & 3 KJV

C.R. Hill, Jr.

# Be By His Love Persuaded

God is a God of matchless love,
His grace – who can comprehend?
His dying upon cruel Calvary's cross,
To forgive humankind of sin!

Yet he does not approve of sin,
Indeed it cost him his dear Son.
Nor will those who chose sin's way,
Be allowed in heaven when life is done.

Repentance is what he requires,
If one is to receive his grace.
One must reject their former ways,
If they wish in the end to see his face.

So hear O children of our time,
Let his love your heart convince.
You cannot climb up heaven's stairs,
If on earth you are on the fence.

––––––––

"But let the righteous be glad: let them rejoice
before God: yea, let them exceedingly rejoice.
4 Sing unto God, sing praises to his name:
extol him that rideth upon the heavens
by his name JAH, and rejoice before him."
Psalm 68: 3 & 4 KJV

## Be Not Dismayed

Disheartened is what I had become,
With so many departing from the Lord.
People losing the vision of what they're to be,
That is so clearly made known in God's word.

It is no use, I thought, to give voice to the news,
For having ears there seems none wants to hear.
It's all noise and lights flashing about,
But no message that is really sincere.

But then I was reminded as I looked at his word,
That God does not leave himself with no one to speak.
Even in whispers his message thunders through time,
For the news of his Son knows no defeat.

"Keep spreading the word," he says unto me,
"For as a witness I am not through with you yet.
Though some seem not to care or hungry to hear,
My message they will not easily forget."

———

"God is faithful, by whom ye were called
unto the fellowship of his Son
Jesus Christ our Lord."
1Corinthians 1: 9 KJV

C.R. Hill, Jr.

# Be Still and Know That I am God

Do I even know what it is to wait,
Or to truly hope in God's word?
Like everyone else I rush through my day,
If God has spoken I am not sure that I heard.

Beside the still waters he restoreth my soul,
So David the Psalmist reminds us.
But who has time for still waters today,
There is far too much worry and fuss.

Lord, slow me down, let me focus on you,
And truly hear what you have to say.
Then lead me along your righteous path,
All through this wonderful day.

Open my mind to whatever you speak,
Let me hide every word in my heart.
Then let my life be fully governed by you,
And never from your word let me part.

————————

"Be still, and know that I am God:
I will be exalted among the heathen,
I will be exalted in the earth."
Psalm 46: 10 KJV

"…they that wait upon the LORD shall
*renew* their strength;
they shall mount up with wings as eagles;
they shall run, and not be weary;
*and* they shall walk, and not faint."
Isaiah 40:31 KJV

## Before The Looking Glass

Once more the time for me arrives,
To take the test before the glass;
Then take a look at the one I see.
What is the reflection that I cast?

Am I true to what I profess,
Does my life express what I believe?
Do others from a distance look,
Is Christ in me what they perceive?

When Jesus washed my sins away,
He put his Spirit in my heart.
Has my life kept to the path,
I then did with Jesus start?

Show me, Lord, if there be things,
That I must yet in me amend,
Lest I forget the grace you've shown,
And no longer walk with you as friend.

———

Read 2Corinthians 13: 5 – 14

"Examine yourselves, whether ye be
in the faith; prove your own selves.
Know ye not your own selves,
how that Jesus Christ is in you,
except ye be reprobates?"
2Corinthians 13: 5 KJV

C.R. Hill, Jr.

# By Faith in Christ Alone

I once saw myself for the sinner I was,
And there Jesus my life transformed.
Yet if now I think myself to be pretty good,
In fact, his grace I now have scorned.

When Jesus we receive by faith,
We through him to sin have died.
Any goodness we then display,
Is then only by his grace supplied.

We ourselves will always sinners be,
Never from our need of grace set free.
It is only because of Jesus' blood,
That God our sins can't see.

Remind me, Jesus, each and every day,
To trust in your grace alone,
And that I can never be good enough,
To for my own sins atone.

———

"For if I build again the things which I destroyed,
I make myself a transgressor. 19 For I through the law
am dead to the law, that I might live unto God.
20 I am crucified with Christ: nevertheless I live;
yet not I, but Christ liveth in me: and the life which
I now live in the flesh I live by the faith of the Son of God,
who loved me, and gave himself for me."
Galatians 2: 18 – 20 KJV

## By His Hand

"He leadeth me, He leadeth me,
By his own hand he leadeth me...."*
Those wonderful words of the hymn,
Call me to the person I want to be.

Day to day in life's struggle and strife,
It is easy to wander astray.
No one has the wisdom to make it alone,
We all need someone to show us the way.

That someone, of course, is Jesus himself,
We are made in the image of his own.
He came among us to show us his way,
And what it is like to be us he has known.

O reach out today and take hold of his hand,
He will walk every step by your side.
He loves you so much he will never forsake,
For your life he was even willing to die.

———

"...he leadeth me in the paths of
righteousness for his name's sake."
Psalm 23:3b KJV

* "He Leadeth Me"
Joseph H. Gilmore
Hymn # 35 *Cokesbury Worship Hymnal*

C.R. Hill, Jr.

# By The Spirit of God

I heard the rocks cry out and speak,
As they sang their praise to the Lord.
O I thought I was something special,
Until I heard from the rocks his Word.

God takes the things that we disregard,
Things simple and to us of no worth,
And he uses these to shame our pride,
As he sheds his grace on the earth.

We tend to think we can do his will,
Yet it is through us that he works.
When we step aside out of his path,
It is just one of those spiritual quirks.

So humble me, Lord –
That like clay in your hand I may be.
Carry me then wherever you will,
Giving others your healing through me.

———

"But God hath chosen the foolish things of the world
to confound the wise; and God hath chosen
the weak things of the world to confound the
things which are mighty; 28 And base things of the world,
and things which are despised, hath God chosen, yea,
and things which are not, to bring to nought things that are;
29 That no flesh should glory in his presence."
1Corinthians 1:27-29 KJV

Read John 9: 1-7 & 1Cor. 1: 27- 29.

## Channels of Blessings

Life that truly lasts is really upside down.
Folks aspire to wealth and fame,
But lives that last give up themselves,
That others through their life may gain.

Most folks think they've naught to give,
If great wealth they do not know,
But those who give the most in life,
Let God's great riches through them flow.

They do not hold God's blessings back,
Or store them up for a rainy day.
Each morn they receive God's gifts afresh,
And cannot wait to give them all away.

These gifts may at the time seem small,
Hardly worth the time they spend.
But the accumulated benefit they have,
Brings great riches at life's end.

———

"And whosoever of you will be the chiefest,
shall be servant of all. 45 For even the Son of man
came not to be ministered unto, but to minister,
and to give his life a ransom for many."
Mark 10: 44 & 45 KJV

C.R. Hill, Jr.

## Christ the Redeemer

O man of finite vision you,
Can you not yet begin to see,
My death upon the cross that day,
Redeemed all that I created to be.

It is I who from everlasting AM,
By whom all that ever was became,
I am the great eternal Word,
Jesus Christ is my eternal name.

When I took upon myself,
The robes of human flesh,
I also assumed into my very soul,
The sin of all creation's mess.

Then on the cross my righteousness,
Did pay the debt of sin's demand.
Yet Sin and Death could not me restrain,
I shall forever reign at God's right hand.

———————

"And they shall teach no more every man his neighbor,
and every man his brother, saying, Know the LORD:
for they shall all know me, from the least of them
unto the greatest of them, saith the Lord: for I will forgive
their iniquity, and I will remember their sin no more."
Jeremiah 31:34 KJV

## Create In Me a Clean Heart

I usually think I'm doing pretty well,
Walking in the way one should.
But every now and then a word blurts out,
I'd refrain from speaking if I could.

The thing that bothers me the most,
About what does from my mouth depart,
Is not the fact that it is common speech,
But that it is a true reflection of my heart.

It reveals that something yet is wrong!
My words expose a shadow that I can't control.
In my heart's dark chambers evil lurketh still,
Spewing out its venom – poisoning my soul!

Then I cry, "Dear Jesus, enter yet again!
By your Holy Spirit please my heart make clean.
Then when my mouth is open, and I begin to speak,
May your holy presence in my words be seen."

---------

"And Jesus said, Are ye also yet without understanding?
17 Do not ye yet understand, that whatsoever entereth in at the mouth
goeth into the belly, and is cast out into the draught?  18 But those
things which proceed out of the mouth come forth from the heart; and
they defile the man."
Matthew 15: 16-18 KJV

"Create in me a clean heart, O God;
and renew a right spirit within me."
Psalm 51: 10 KJV

## Distinct

What sets us apart from others,
If not the presence of the Lord?
If not that we commune with Jesus,
God with us, the eternal Word?

If not that he does us surround,
Daily with his saving grace,
Hiding us within the Rock of Ages,
Covering there our sin's disgrace?

We have no reason in ourselves,
To think that we any different are,
From any other folks on earth,
Who from God have wandered far.

But in his mercy God has claimed us,
And sent us Jesus to save our soul,
So long as we shall embrace his mercy,
And yield our lives to his control.

This it is that sets us apart,
That in us God's love do others see,
As we with Jesus daily walk,
And like him in nature strive to be.

---

Read Exodus 33: 12 – 23

"For wherein shall it be known here that
I and thy people have found grace in thy sight?
Is it not in that thou goest with us? so shall we be separated,
I and thy people, from all the people that are
upon the face of the earth."
Exodus 33: 16 KJV

## Empty Vessels

The plantings of the Lord,
Are strange and marvelous things.
They are the very presence,
From which his wonder springs.

They are themselves as nothing,
No things one should desire.
They are as common bushes,
Yet ablaze with holy fire.

To and fro throughout creation,
They move about almost unseen,
So ordinarily common they,
The world does them as nothing deem.

But God in his great wisdom,
Does their empty status use,
To bring down the power of nations,
And to make his creation new.

––––––––

"But God hath chosen the foolish things of the world
to confound the wise; and God hath chosen
the weak things of the world to confound the
things which are mighty; 28 And base things of the world,
and things which are despised, hath God chosen, yea,
and things which are not, to bring to nought things that are;
29 That no flesh should glory in his presence."
1Corinthians 1:27-29 KJV

C.R. Hill, Jr.

## Equipped By the Spirit

Let your life by God's Spirit be led,
Follow not your fleshly desire.
Those who with Jesus walk,
Are called to a lifestyle higher.

Be not lured by things that shine,
Or be seduced by the culture's sin,
Satin's ways appear inviting and sweet,
But death alone is their journey's end.

Jesus has come to free you from death,
By his Spirit he equips you with power.
Follow him in the way of the cross,
Rise to your best in your destiny's hour.

Face with courage life's challenging task,
Be strong in resolve to evil resist.
Jesus your leader within you resides,
To, in your weakness, lend his assist.

———————

Read 1Corinthians 12; 1 -11

"But all these [gifts of the Spirit] worketh
that one and the selfsame Spirit, dividing to
every man severally as he will."
1Corinthians 12: 11 KJV

## Find the Rhythm for the Race

"Find the rhythm of reliance,
Match your cadence to my Son.
Then you will climb the steepest grades,
And reach my summit when day is done.

Many climbers try with power,
The mountains of this life to climb,
But by the wayside they fall exhausted,
To the mountain's victory they resign.

Yet the ones who make the grade,
Who cross the finish line of the race,
Are they who along the way,
Have had the faith to match my pace.

In the split-stream of my Son,
By the power of love and grace,
They match the tempo of my Spirit,
And on my podium they take their place."

———————

"Be ye therefore followers of God, as dear children;
2 And walk in love, as Christ also hath loved us,
and hath given himself for us an offering and
a sacrifice to God for a sweetsmelling savour."
Ephesians 5: 1 & 2 KJV

C.R. Hill, Jr.

## Finding Life's Way

I see the cluttered ways of the world,
Looking like spaghetti in a bowl;
Then wonder how one is ever to find,
The way to life's highest goal.

So many sighs, so many cry out,
A bedlam of voices I hear!
Which path to take – how do I choose?
To which should my soul adhere?

I see a road broad and well paved,
I see many are traveling thereon.
But looking ahead to that road's end,
I note that all of those travelers are gone.

I see a path through yonder narrow gate,
Little traveled for it is rugged and steep.
Yet looking ahead I see life's greatest goal,
Is reached if one to this pathway will keep.

––––––––––

"O that my ways were directed to keep thy statutes!
6 Then shall I not be ashamed, when I have
respect unto all thy commandments."
Psalm 119: 5 & 6 KJV

"Jesus saith unto him [Thomas] I am the way,
the truth, and the life: no man cometh
unto the Father, but by me."
John 14:6 KJV

"…but this one thing I do, forgetting those things
which are behind, and reaching forth unto those things
which are before, 14 I press toward the mark
for the prize of the high calling
of God in Christ Jesus."
Philippians 3:13b – 14 KJV

33

## Firm In Your Faith

It is God's desire for every life,
To become a match to his.
And for his likeness to find expression,
Right where each person lives.

The tempter tries to defeat this goal,
And steer God's followers wrong.
So one must the more diligent be,
To focus on Jesus all day long.

It is in this darkened world we find,
The greatest need for God's pure light.
That is why the Prince of Darkness,
Does so against God's followers fight.

Therefore, my brothers and sisters too,
You must at all times be on alert.
For the devil's deepest desire,
Is to your pure witness hurt.

--------

"Casting all your care upon him; for he careth for you.
8 Be sober, be vigilant; because your adversary the devil,
as a roaring lion, walketh about, seeking whom he may devour:
9 Whom resist stedfast in the faith, knowing that the same afflictions
are accomplished in your brethren that are in the world."
1Peter 5: 7 - 9 KJV

# Firstfruits

Clay we were, and clay we are,
And clay we will always be,
Without God's hand upon our soul,
Who from clay's bondage sets us free.

Into our souls his breath of life,
Makes to us his presence known,
And fills us with his redeeming love,
As he claims us for his own.

It is not to set us upon some shelf,
To be admired by him each day.
He formed us for his kingdom's use,
In reaching other hearts of clay.

We are the firstfruits of redeeming grace,
That is transforming sin's darkened world.
God refines us with his Spirit's fire,
Then we are as lights into the darkness hurled.

––––––––––

"Of his own will begat he us with the word of truth,
that we should be a kind of firstfruits of his creatures."
James 1:18 KJV

"…know ye not that your body is the temple
of the Holy Ghost which is in you, which ye have of God,
and ye are not your own? 20 For ye are bought with a price:
therefore glorify God in your body, and in your spirit, which are
God's."
1Corinthians 6: 19 & 20 KJV

## Follow the Right Pattern

I laced a wheel the other day,
Running spokes from a hub to a rim,
A dozen times I laced it up wrong,
And had to start all over again.

I finally saw where my problem lay,
I was following the wrong pattern to start.
Now lacing a wheel is like building a life,
One needs the right pattern for the heart.

There is many a way to get it all wrong,
I've learned that the hard way myself.
Some follow a pattern for pleasure or fame,
Others choose a pattern for wealth.

Yet the only pattern that gets it right,
Is the one that God has for you.
That Pattern is found in Jesus his Son,
Build on him for a life that is true.

---

"…he [Jesus] said unto them, Know ye what I have done to you? 13 ye
call me Master and Lord: and ye say well; for *so* I am. 14 If I then, *your*
Lord and Master, have washed your feet;
ye also ought to wash one another's feet. 15 For I have given
you an example, that ye should do as I have done to you."
John 13:12b – 15 KJV

"Jesus saith unto him… follow thou me."
John 21:22 KJV

C.R. Hill, Jr.

# For A Life as God Designs

A widow once was gathering sticks,
To go home and build a fire.
Whereupon her final meal to cook,
Then with her son expire.

But the man of God did meet here there,
And asked she bake for him a cake,
And bring him a little water too.
For God your meal to last will make.

So many times in life we find,
Ourselves at our wit's end,
Then turn to God in simple faith,
And he renews our hope again.

For life we're told in Jesus' words,
Is more than food or drink,
It is more than all material things,
As the world would have us think.

Life that really satisfies the soul,
That overcomes the hardest times,
Is that which comes from trusting God,
For our life as he designs.

---

Read 1Kings 17:8-16

"Therefore take no thought, saying, What shall we eat?
or, What shall we drink? or, Wherewithal shall we be clothed?
32 (For after all these things do the Gentiles seek:) for your
heavenly Father knoweth that ye have need of all these things.
33 But seek ye first the kingdom of God, and his righteousness;
and all these things shall be added unto you."
Matthew 6: 31-33 KJV

## Forgiving the Stinging Blows

Life sometimes deals us stinging blows,
That crush our will to live.
Then all that is within us wants revenge;
While the Bible says forgive.

How are we, such mortal folks,
To suppress our passions' cry?
Forgo our right to set things straight?
Our pride would rather die!

But then in anguish, pain and grief,
We see Jesus on the tree,
And we hear him cry, "I forgive them all,
For what they did to me."

So what of us who profess in faith,
Our claim to follow him,
Shall we thus bow to lesser drives,
Or forgive and live again?

———————

"Put on therefore, as the elect of God, holy and beloved,
bowels of mercies, kindness, humbleness of mind, meekness,
longsuffering;
13 Forbearing one another, and forgiving one another,
if any man have a quarrel against any; even as
Christ forgave you, so also do ye."
Colossians 3: 12 & 13 KJV

C.R. Hill, Jr.

## From Out of Darkness Called

I once lived in darkness,
Thinking that my life was doing fine;
Little did I know how far,
I had strayed from God's design.

Until one day it hit me,
I had to face myself in shame.
I had really done an excellent job,
Of smearing mud upon my name.

There in my valley dark with guilt,
My soul could not find relief,
Until God's grace like a shaft of light,
Bathed my heart in true belief.

I knew at once what scripture meant;
Jesus had died for all my sin!
I felt the cleansing of forgiveness,
As his arms received me in.

———————

"But ye are a chosen generation, a royal priesthood,
an holy nation, a peculiar people; that ye should
shew forth the praises of him who hath called
you out of darkness into his marvellous light:"
1Peter 2: 9 KJV

I Talked With Him This Morning

## From Out Of Deep Waters

Troubled waters roar about me,
Their waves would have me drown,
But the Master of the sea,
Says that he will never let me down.

He will save when naught else can,
Nor when no one even cares,
He is the silent presence about me,
Who answers all my prayers.

O when the storm is raging so,
And all about is dark,
He will hide me beneath his wing,
And keep me safe within his ark.

So I'll trust him throughout my life,
For his promises do forever stand,
And when my voyage on earth is o'er
I shall hold fast to his guiding hand.

---

"But the meek shall inherit the earth,
And shall delight themselves in the abundance of peace."
Psalm 37: 11 KJV

" 27 But God hath chosen the foolish things of the world to confound
the wise; and God hath chosen the weak things of the world to
confound the things which are mighty; 28 And base things of the world,
and things which are despised, hath God chosen, yea, and things which
are not, to bring to nought things that are:"
1Corinthians. 1:28 KJV

40

C.R. Hill, Jr.

## From The Shallow Eddies' Capture

Like an autumn leaf on a forest stream,
I drift in the eddies of the shallows,
I avoid the rush of rapid's shoots,
And the deeper pools God hallows.

Life is peaceful in shallow places,
There no dangers are incurred.
It requires no effort just to float around,
There no calls from God are heard.

Of course like leaves in the shallow edges,
Of a forest stream that's flowing swift,
A life spent floating in the shallows,
Never knows the depth of God's great gift.

Therefore I'll pray God's Holy Spirit,
By his wind will sweep me free,
From the shallow eddies' capture,
So I the depths of God may see.

––––––––––

"Let the words of my mouth, and the meditation
of my heart, be acceptable in thy sight,
O LORD, my strength, and my redeemer."
Psalm 19: 14 KJV

## Fully Rely On God

"Sufficient unto the day,
The evil thereof is."
We always hear Jesus saying,
Each day its own trouble gives.

And while I do agree,
There is truth in that aplenty;
Yet if our resources are sufficient,
On God we'll not depend for any.

It seems to me the greater evil,
Is to go through each day relying,
Not on our heavenly Father,
To be all our needs supplying.

Of course we must act wisely,
Using well the gifts he does supply,
But we always must remember,
That without his gifts of grace we die.

———

Read Luke 12: 13 – 21

"Take therefore no thought for the morrow:
for the morrow shall take thought for the
things of itself.  Sufficient unto the day
*is* the evil thereof."
Matthew 6: 34 KJV

C.R. Hill, Jr.

## Fully Trusting God

O how often the man in me,
Forgets on whom I must rely,
And holds back from trusting God,
To be my full supply.

I think I'll give a generous sum,
His mission to achieve,
But hold back a bit of tithe,
And fail his blessings to receive.

Not that I can his blessing buy,
If willingly the full tithe I give,
It is rather that full tithe reflects,
How deep in faith I really live.

The same applies in all of life,
In all of my daily walk.
When I fully trust in God,
God backs with acts my talk.

———————

"Bring ye all the tithes into the storehouse,
that there may be meat in mine house,
and prove me now herewith, saith the LORD of hosts,
if I will not open you the windows of heaven,
and pour you out a blessing, that *there shall* not
*be room* enough *to receive it*.."
Malachi 3:10 KJV

## Gaining Perspective

O how my children spend their time,
On all life's minor things,
And let themselves get all worked up,
Over that which no peace brings.

When all that really matters most,
Is first they spend some time with me,
Then the earthly cares they face,
Would not so dreaded be.

Perspective!
That is the thing to gain,
Everything is changed when first,
Your day is started in my name.

Hear me now my child,
Mark well the words I say,
Leave off putting the trivial things,
At the beginning of your day.

---

"But seek ye first the kingdom of God,
and his righteousness; and all these things
shall be added unto you."
Matthew 6:33 KJV

C.R. Hill, Jr.

# Gershom*

I met a man named "Gershom,"
It meant sojourner in a foreign land.
Indeed I see Gershoms every day,
As beside their beds I stand.

I serve among the sick and ill,
In a place of healing grace,
Yet it is a foreign land to those,
Who spend a while within that place.

The Psalmist said it's hard to sing,
When the soul is away from home,
So I try to help them sing while there,
By making God's presence to them known.

There is no land so far away,
No Babylon of your soul,
That God's presence is missing there,
Or his love not in control.

So if today you feel your name is changed,
And by Gershom your are now known,
Let me reassure you friend,
God is with you – you are not alone.

---

Read Psalm 137: 1 -4 and Psalm 139: 1 – 112
"How shall we sing the LORD'S song in a strange land?"
Psalm 137: 4 KJV
"Whither shall I go from thy spirit
Or whither shall I flee from thy presence?
8 If I ascend up into heaven, thou art there:
If I make my bed in hell, behold, thou art there.
9 If I take the wings of the morning, and dwell
in the utter most parts of the sea;  10 Even there shall
thy hand lead me, and thy right hand shall hold me."
Psalm 139: 7 - 10 KJV
*Gershom: see Exodus 2: 21 & 22

## Get Out Of The Boat

Old Peter was scared like his brothers that night,
When Jesus came walking by;
Out on the sea in the midst of a storm,
Yet Jesus walked high and dry.

They cried out in fright at the unusual sight,
A man walking were he'd be lucky to swim.
But Jesus replied, "Let your hearts have no fear",
Then bid old Peter to walk out to Him.

Peter stepped out without giving a thought,
And with eyes fixed on Jesus he strolled.
But his faith became weak when he thought of the wind,
Then saw how the sea billows rolled.

"Help me!" he cried as he started to sink,
"Lord, take my hand lest I die!"
Of course Jesus caught hold and took him back safe,
Not entirely displeased with his try.

True, he started to sink in the turbulent brine,
But his friends had no reason to gloat,
For when Jesus said "come" on the water that night,
At least old Peter got out of the boat.

––––––––––

Read Matthew 14:22-32

"And immediately Jesus stretched forth *his* hand,
and caught him, and said unto him, O thou of little faith,
wherefore didst thou doubt?"
Matthew 14: 31 KJV

C.R. Hill, Jr.

## Get Suited Up

I've stepped out on a dangerous path,
If I had forgotten my belt to wear,
I would be exposed as a joke,
Like a fool standing bare.

If I had left off my vest,
There would not be any need,
For the enemy I meet,
To pay me any heed.

Without the right shoes,
I would be unable to stand,
For the ground under me,
Would be all shifting sand.

And so it is with the armor of God,
Each piece I much need,
From the belt to the sword,
If in following Jesus I am to succeed.

———————

Read Ephesians 6:10-17

"Finally, my brethren, be strong in the Lord,
and in the power of his might. 11 Put on the whole armour of God,
that ye may be able to stand against the wiles of the devil."
Ephesians 6: 10 & 11 KJV

## God's Yonder Waiting Shore

A river flows  from the throne of God,
Dividing shores of time from those forevermore,
And the march of each day's sun,
Closer brings yonder waiting shore.

This present realm in which we live,
Is but the proving ground,
For the life that yonder waits,
When we our robes of time lay down.

Yet most who dwell within time's span,
See not what lies beyond tomorrow.
They spend their days pursuing things,
That in the end will only lead to sorrow.

While those who see with eyes of faith,
Are not blind to the distant view.
They give themselves to living now,
For the things forever true.

Always the time does quickly come,
For passing through life's temporal door.
The question is, will then you ready be,
For life on God's yonder waiting shore?

———————

"For now we see through a glass, darkly;
but then face to face: now I know in part;
but then shall I know even as also I am known.
13 And now abideth faith, hope, charity, these three;
but the greatest of these *is* charity."
1Corinthians 13: 12 & 13 KJV

C.R. Hill, Jr.

# God's Spirit's Lengthy Stride

Out upon the trail of life,
I marched in rank one day,
Thinking as I marched along,
There's a debt for life to pay.

Determined I right then and there,
I would my obligation meet;
Yet I for all my best intent,
Was fast bound for deep defeat.

It was then that grace did intervene,
For Jesus covered all my sin.
Through his Spirit's renewing power,
My life's page was clean again.

Now for me the debt is changed;
As to God's grace I am obliged;
To match my steps along life's trail,
With God's Spirit's lengthy stride."

————————

"For as many as are led by the Spirit of God,
they are the sons of God.  15 For ye have not received
the spirit of bondage again to fear; but ye have received
the Spirit of adoption, whereby we cry, 'Abba, Father.'"
Romans 8: 14 & 15 KJV

49

## God's Time Change

The night of sin has long prevailed,
Covering with darkness the human soul.
But light has dawned in Jesus Christ,
Who accomplishes God's salvation's goal.

So awake O sleeper from sin daze slumber,
Open your eyes to God's new day.
Why linger longer beneath darkness' cover,
Or go about in sin's thick haze?

Jesus has brought the light of grace,
That sets free the sin-stained heart,
He cleanses with his righteous blood,
Giving the soul a brand new start.

Wake up!  Salvation's day has dawned!
Cast off the nightclothes of sins past.
Open wide the blinds upon your heart,
Behold your Savior is here at last.

———

"The people which sat in darkness saw great light;
and to them which sat in the region and shadow
of death light is sprung up."
Matthew 4: 16 KJV

C.R. Hill, Jr.

## He Restoreth My Soul

I once walked a road like this,
With Patches at my side,
He'd run and dart in search of quail,
As they'd attempt to hide.

Gone long now are the days,
When we would have such fun.
When I would walk such roads as these,
With hunting dog and gun.

Now roads like these are hard to find,
Amid malls and sprawling towns,
Where pastures green and waters still,
Can yet by the soul be found.

So today as I walk this quiet road,
In the morning sunshine fair,
I feed my mind upon God's Word,
And he my soul restoreth there.

———————

"He restoreth my soul: he leadeth me in the paths
of righteousness for his name's sake."
Psalm 23: 3 KJV

## Heaven's Path

Across the churning evening sea,
Rides a full moon's sparkling shaft,
That comes to rest right at my feet,
Like a heavenward leading path.

As I stroll along the shores of time,
The moon's rays seem to follow me;
Whenever I chance to seaward glance,
It shines like a highway upon the sea.

Across the storm-tossed human lives,
Shines the Savior's beaming love,
That comes to rest at each person's feet,
Like a bright highway from above.

All who turn and step out with faith,
Upon the beam God's love has cast,
Will walk upon life's storm-tossed sea,
For Jesus Christ will be their path.

---

"Jesus saith unto him [Thomas], I am the way,
the truth, and the life: no man cometh unto the Father,
but by me. 7 If ye had known me, ye should have
known my Father also: and from henceforth
ye know him, and have seen him."
John 14: 6 & 7 KJV

C.R. Hill, Jr.

# Heaven's Dressing Room

What gives the Christian voice to sing,
When death doth fling its arrow?
What gives the Christian courage to walk,
Through the shadowed valley narrow?

How in the face of death's cold grasp,
Can the Christian still believe,
That death is but the thin veiled hoax,
Used by the devil to deceive?

Ah, here the answer lies my friend,
In the garden's empty tomb,
For Jesus converted the dreaded grave,
Into heaven's dressing room.

So ask again from whence it comes,
The Christian's courage brave,
It comes because in Jesus Christ,
We have overcome the grave!

---

"Jesus said unto her, 'I am the resurrection,
and the life: he that believeth in me,
though he were dead, yet shall he live:
26 And whosoever liveth and believeth in me
shall never die. Believest thou this?"
John 11:25 & 26 KJV

## Heroes on Hillsides

Heroes on hillsides,
White headstones all aligned,
These for their country,
Their lives have all resigned.

We hold them each in honor,
Though we know not every name,
And we lift them up to heaven,
So thankful that they came.

Then turn we from those hillsides,
To the nation that they served,
Does she still honor their ideals,
Or has she from that pathway swerved?

O let us anew remember
To honor these heroes every day,
By making sure our nation
Does her true path stay.

———

"The LORD bringeth the counsel of the heathen to nought:
he maketh the devices of the people of none effect.
11 The counsel of the LORD standeth for ever, the thoughts
of his heart to all generations. 12 Blessed is the nation
whose God is the LORD; and the people whom he hath
chosen for his own inheritance."
Psalm 33: 10 -12 KJV

C.R. Hill, Jr.

# His Faithful Follower Will You Be?

What God has done to save our souls,
Goes far beyond belief.
Not only has he forgiven our past,
We are now from sin's power released.

Washed we've been in the blood of Christ,
Then sanctified by his grace,
We've been justified in the name of Jesus,
That one day we may see God's face.

Why then fall back into former ways,
Or be lured onto the carnal trail?
Do not be deceived by sin's allures,
Lest you at following Jesus fail.

It is grace through faith in Christ alone,
That gives us hope to heaven gain,
But once in faith we've turned to him,
We are to live faithful to his name.

————

"Know ye not that the unrighteous
shall not inherit the kingdom of God?
Be not deceived: neither fornicators,
nor idolaters, nor adulterers, nor effeminate,
nor abusers of themselves with mankind,
10 Nor thieves, nor covetous, nor drunkards,
nor revilers, nor extortioners,
shall inherit the kingdom of God. 11 And such
were some of you: but ye are washed, but ye are
sanctified, but ye are justified in the name of the
Lord Jesus, and by the Spirit of our God."
1Corinthians 6: 9 – 11 KJV

I Talked With Him This Morning

## His Light That Shines Within

Doomed I was to the downward track,
Of the broad well-traveled way,
Where the masses take the gloomy trip,
Beyond all reach of day.

The passage booked, the time arrived,
My fate seemed already sealed,
Until God's grace did intervene,
With the bread of life revealed.

O Bread of Life, O sacred Loaf,
O Food that saves the soul,
O blessed Savior Jesus Christ,
Who returns the lost to heaven's fold.

Come ye now to his out stretched hand,
Receive the gift of life from him,
Then let the world behold in you,
His light that shines within.

————

"But ye *are* a chosen generation, a royal priesthood,
an holy nation, a peculiar people; that ye should shew forth
the praises of him who hath called you out of darkness
into his marvellous light: 10 Which in time past *were* not
a people, but *are* now the people of God: which had not
obtained mercy, but not have obtained mercy."
1Peter 2: 9 & 10 KJV

C.R. Hill, Jr.

# His Likeness to Fulfill

Two things that faith in Christ involve,
Are fear and action taken.
When Jesus enters into one's heart,
He does in us a righteous will awaken.

The fear is not the grip of horror,
That overtakes those who have no faith;
It is the overwhelming awesome wonder,
Felt by all who will receive his grace.

That fear does rearrange the heart.
It creates in the soul a righteous will;
That causes those who in Jesus trust
His likeness to fulfill.

Then in their living through each day,
They seek to do what is just and right;
To following all the ways of Jesus,
And fill the world with heaven's light.

———————

"Then Peter opened his mouth, and said,
Of a truth I perceive that God is no respecter of persons:
35 But in every nation he that feareth him,
and worketh righteousness, is accepted with him."
Acts 10:34 & 35 KJV

## His Word

"I wait for the Lord, my soul waits,
And in his word I hope;"*
This is the foundation upon which I rest,
Desiring to fathom his word in full scope.

His Word, the expression of his divine being,
Brought into existence all of creation,
His Word then incarnate in Jesus The Christ,
Delivers us from sin by his great salvation.

It is his Word from eternity to eternity again,
That Word that can never, no never be broken,
My soul is renewed in the Word's shelter,
Feeding on every word he has spoken.

O come to God's manna, his life giving Word,
There eat the bread freely as your life it renews.
Then taking his Word with you, go into the world,
Sharing with others from his Word the good news.

———————

*"I wait for the LORD, my soul doth wait,
and in his word do I hope."
Psalm 130: 5 KJV

C.R. Hill, Jr.

## Hold Fast the Hope

"O my child of wondering mind,
Can you not for an hour look at me?
Focus here upon my face,
That you true life in it may see.

I know it is your heart's desire,
To walk faithfully with me and true,
Yet present are those other things,
Seeking to come between me and you.

Come away for a while with me,
Leave those things that seek your heart.
Hear my voice; let it speak to you,
Don't let the world pull us apart.

Then you shall be my sharpened tool,
Who in my hand will never turn,
But completes the task I call you to,
That of my salvation the lost may learn.

———————

"Having therefore, brethren, boldness to enter into the holiest
by the blood of Jesus, 20 By a new and living way, which he
hath consecrated for us, through the veil, that is to say, his flesh; 21
And *having* an high priest over the house of God; 22 Let us draw near
with a true heart in full assurance of faith, having our hearts sprinkled
from an evil conscience, and our bodies washed with pure water. 23
Let us hold fast the profession of *our* faith without wavering;
(for he is faithful that promised;)…"
Hebrews 10: 19-23 KJV

## Hope For Our Valleys Of Bones

I often walk through a valley of bones,
Among people whose hope is all gone.
Then to the Lord I must again turn,
For a word that will give them a song.

For God is not dead nor indifferent is he,
To the woes that beset us down here,
He knows our pain in the valley of bones,
With compassion he notes our each tear.

True we are weak and unable to rise,
And our valley of bones we can't change.
But he is the Almighty – the God over all,
And new life for our bones he'll arrange.

So when you are in that desolate state,
And feel you can no longer hold on,
Turn to Jesus who from the valley has risen,
And he will place in your heart a new song.

––––––––––

"Then he said unto me, Son of man, these bones
are the whole house of Israel: behold, they say,
Our bones are dried , and our hope is lost:
we are cut off from our parts. 12 Therefore prophesy
and say unto them, Thus saith the Lord God; Behold,
O my people, I will open your graves, and cause you to come
up out of your graves, and bring you into the land of Israel."
Ezekiel 37: 11 & 12 KJV

"The Lord *is* my strength and song;
is become my salvation."
Psalm 118: 14 KJV

# C.R. Hill, Jr.

## I Talked With Him This Morning

I talked with Him this morning,
And do you know what he said?
He said, "I am right down here beside you,
You have nothing now to dread.

I know the road you're traveling,
Now through a rough stretch you must go,
If I am going to use you,
To let my grace to lost souls show.

I know it won't be easy,
You will want to turn aside,
But you always must remember,
For this road you're on I died.

So hang in there my servant,
And faithful to God be,
For as the outcome of your calling,
Many souls will heaven see."

---

"*We are* troubled on every side, yet not distressed;
*we are* perplexed, but not in despair; 9 Persecuted,
but not forsaken; cast down, but not destroyed;
10 Always bearing about in the body the dying
of the Lord Jesus, that the life also of Jesus
might be made manifest in our body."
2Corinthians 4: 8-10 KJV

## In As Much

I work with people everyday,
Who for the sick do care,
They give themselves with endless grace,
That patients may the better fare.

With caring hands and kindly words,
They give encouragement and hope,
Even when the needs they face,
Are beyond their efforts' scope.

When the outcome goes not their way,
They yet must to other sick attend,
Not letting what has just transpired,
Their very best amend.

Yet day by day deep in their hearts,
The tears they've felt reside,
As they their special kinship share,
With Jesus Christ who died.

Oh look to Jesus each day my friends.
In his presence always stay,
And when your heart does heavy grow,
Let him wipe your tears away.

———

Read Matthew 25: 31-46

"And the King shall answer and say unto them,
Verily I say unto you, Inasmuch as ye have done
*it* unto one of the least of these my brethren,
ye have done *it* unto me."
Matthew 25:40 KJV

C.R. Hill, Jr.

## In Christ Shall All Be Made Alive

So hard we try to do what's right,
To live the upright life,
But then our focus is distracted,
By all of the daily strife.

We look around at other folks,
And think, "Oh, well, we're not so bad."
When we see the way they live,
We ask, "How can God with us be mad?"

Of course this is to miss the point,
Of God's great salvation's grace.
There is nothing we can do to earn it,
But look into the risen Jesus' face.

Jesus accomplished it for us all,
By bearing our sins on Calvary's cross.
Then when he rose up from the dead,
He secured eternal life for us the lost.

––––––––––

"But now is Christ risen from the dead,
*and* become the firstfruits of them that slept. 21
For since by man came death, by man *came* also
the resurrection of the dead. 22 For as in Adam all die,
even so in Christ shall all be made alive."
1Corinthians 15:20 -22 KJV

63

I Talked With Him This Morning

## In His Abiding Grace

When I've strayed from the path,
And found myself alone,
Away from fellowship with Christ,
Feeling strictly on my own.

Then stopped to recognize my fault,
And turned to find Christ there,
I've found it hard to accept his love,
Or his forgiveness of my error.

Yet his grace beyond all belief,
Still covers all my sin,
So when I reach and take his hand,
He lets me walk with him again.

O my lost and sin sick friend,
Please learn from what I say,
Jesus' love reaches out to you,
To wash all your sins away.

So take his hand without delay,
And you too will walk with him.
Then clean and whole you too shall be,
As other souls to Christ you'll win.

---

"And when he came to himself, he said, How many hired servants of my father's have bread enough and to spare, and I perish with hunger! 18 I will arise and go to my father, and will say unto him, Father, I have sinned against heaven, and before thee, 19 And am no more worthy to be called thy son: make me as one of thy hired servants. 20 And he arose, and came to his father. But when he was yet a great way off, his father saw him, and had compassion, and ran, and fell on his neck, and kissed him."
Luke 15: 17 – 20 KJV

C.R. Hill, Jr.

# In Secret Meet Christ at the Well

She went to the well with a secret to hide,
Of her shame, and the public's scorn.
There at the well – her secret revealed,
She experienced her spirit reborn.

She went out to the well at noontime,
For she thought she would be all alone.
There were things she'd rather not deal with,
Though her failures to all were well known.

At the well she encountered a stranger,
Who asked for a drink from her hand.
Then offered her water from heaven,
In place of water from a hole in the sand.

She went to the well with a secret to hide,
And she left with a secret to tell,
Of the change in a life that can happen,
When in secret one meets Christ at the well.

———————

Read John 4: 5-42

"Jesus answered and said unto her,
If thou knewest the gift of God, and who it is
that saith to thee, Give me to drink; thou wouldest
have asked of him, and he would have
given thee living water."
John 4: 10 KJV

65

I Talked With Him This Morning

## In The Mind of Jesus

What is the mission we have in life?
What purpose should we fulfill?
To become like Jesus in every way,
That is our heavenly Father's will.

Yet what does it mean like Jesus to be?
Are we to look and dress like him?
Those who Elvis do imitate,
Dress to make us think he lives again.

Of course that is not the thing at all,
When like Jesus we seek to be.
It is his nature we are to match,
That others his character in us may see.

It is walking close in fellowship,
As in his words we his person discern,
And living daily by faith and love,
That we may his nature and character learn.

Then in us his fruits do ripen,
At a quiet yet steady pace,
Until when others look upon our lives,
They begin to discern his face.

———

"Let this mind be in you, which was also in Christ Jesus:
6 Who, being in the form of God, thought it not robbery to
be equal with God: 7 But made himself of no reputation,
and took upon him the form of a servant, and was made
in the likeness of men: 8 And being found in fashion as
a man, he humbled himself, and became obedient unto
death, even the death of the cross."
Philippians 2: 5-8 KJV

## In The Path of Righteousness

Though holiness be not the path,
That one must take to God,
It is the product of that life,
For all who God's path do trod.

For one cannot be by Christ,
A soul he has made alive,
And still live by the sinful ways,
In which they once did thrive.

The love of Jesus changes things,
In the heart and soul of all,
Who in repentance receive his grace,
And who daily on him call.

So check yourself each day at dawn,
Is it the path of light you walk,
Do the things you do each day,
Match the faith you talk?

---

"…walk as children of light: 9 (For the fruit
of the Spirit is in all goodness and righteousness
and truth;) 10 Proving what is acceptable unto the Lord."
Ephesians 5:8b – 10 KJV,

I Talked With Him This Morning

## Into The Hands of Jesus

A net there has been laid for me,
A trap to do me in!
Yet through the pit that evil digs,
My redeemer's grace will win.

Its painful sting I'll surely feel,
Its horrible sight I'll see,
Yet from its grip at the day's end,
My God will set me free.

The powers of death cannot contain,
Nor can evil win the day,
When a soul puts their trust in Christ,
Making Jesus their chosen way.

He'll lift me up on eagle's wings,
New strength my legs will gain.
For I have placed all my trust in him,
And followed faithfully in his name.

———

"For thou *art* my rock and my fortress; therefore
for thy name's sake lead me, and guide me.
4 Pull me out of the net that they have laid privily
for me: for thou *art* my strength.  5 Into thine hand
I commit my spirit: thou hast redeemed me,
O Lord God of truth."
Psalm 31: 3 – 5 KJV

C.R. Hill, Jr.

## Is God Telling Us Something?

Today I look out and I see a world,
All covered with ice and snow.
No cars are filling the roads anywhere,
Planes and buses can't even go.

But does anyone ask just why this is,
Does anyone have even a clue?
Why storms and disasters aplenty,
Disrupt the things we want to do?

Look back for a moment on times of old,
When God's people turned from God's ways.
He sent them droughts, and locusts and more,
Yet they still refused to include him in their days.

No nation can stand on its own very long,
They will quickly fall down in a heap,
If they keep refusing to seek him as The Lord,
And his will and commands not keep.

―――――――

"But what things were gain to me, those I counted loss
for Christ. 8 Yea doubtless, and I count al things but
loss for the excellency of the knowledge of Christ Jesus
my Lord: for whom I have suffered the loss of all things,
and do count them but dung, that I may win Christ,…
15 Let us therefore, as many as be perfect, be thus minded:…."
Philippians 3: 7-8 & 15a KJV

I Talked With Him This Morning

## Let Jesus Fill Your Tank.

As empty as a dried up well,
That is how I often feel.
It is then when I the most,
Must to God's word appeal.

It is his promise to with us be,
And forgive us when we repent.
It is for our empty souls to fill,
That Jesus Christ is sent.

We have no price within our hands,
There is no payment that we can make.
God fills us with his righteousness,
For his dear Son's own sake.

So let your empty soul be still,
Wait at God's river bank,
There by God's loving grace,
Let Jesus fill your tank.

———————

"And he that sat upon the throne said,
Behold, I make all things new. And he
said unto me, Write: for these words are true
and faithful. 6 And he said unto me, It is done.
I am Alpha and Omega, the beginning and the end.
I will give unto him that is athirst of the fountain
of the water of life freely. 7 He that overcometh
shall inherit all things; and I will be his God,
and he shall be my son."
Revelation 21:5-7 KJV

C.R. Hill, Jr.

## Let the Lamps of Love Be Burning

A person can be so far away from God,
That they do not even know they are lost.
They have not a clue how great is their need,
Or of the redemption Jesus bought at such cost.

That is the condition of many in our world,
Sin's night is so dark they can't see,
That Jesus has come and died on the cross,
So they can from sin's darkness be free.

Need Jesus have greater reason than this,
To make of his followers the light?
So trim your wick and clean your globe,
The world waits for you to shatter sin's night.

Let Jesus' love be seen in all that you do,
Love is the power by which the lost you will win.
And you will be amazed before heaven's gates,
At all the lost souls your lantern led in.

————

"Ye are the light of the world. A city that is set
on a hill cannot be hid. 15 Neither do men light
a candle, and put it under a bushel, but on a candlestick;
and it giveth light unto all that are in the house. 16 Let
your light so shine before men, that they may see your
good works, and glorify your Father which is in heaven."
Matthew 5:14-16 KJV

## Let The Thunder Roll

I see the towering mountains,
I behold the raging seas,
I hear the thundering voice,
Of the Lord over all of these.

I look at the world around me,
Where mankind is going mad,
Yet hear no thunder of God's voice,
And that I find to be very sad.

Then God whispers in my ear,
Or rather deep within my heart,
"My word is in my people's hands,
Let My people the thunder start."

"Let not fear cause them their tongue to hold,
Thinking they for me may misspeak.
Let them yield to my Spirit's lead,
As my will they truly seek."

---

Read Psalms 29
Isaiah 61: 1-4 &
Acts 8:14-17

"The Spirit of the Lord God is upon me;
because the Lord hath anointed me
to preach good tidings unto the meek;
he hath sent me to bind up the brokenhearted,
to proclaim liberty to the captives,
and the opening of the prison
to them that are bound:"
Isaiah 61:1 KJV

"…as my Father hath sent me, even so send I you."
John 20: 21 KJV

72

C.R. Hill, Jr.

## Let the Truth Be Told

When Jesus before his accusers stood,
And was asked what he had said,
He told them he has openly spoken,
"Ask those who heard instead."

Now we are often by doubters faced,
Who have the message all wrong.
Disbelief has closed their minds,
They don't hear the Gospel song.

Then we are the ones to witness bear,
To the truth that Jesus taught,
And shine the light of his good news,
That to this darkened world he brought.

Oh there will always doubters be,
Who will rile against his word,
So we must the more faithful be,
To tell the truth we have heard.

———

Read John 18:19 -24.

"Then said Jesus to those Jews which believed on him,
If ye continue in my word, *then* are ye my disciples indeed;"
John 8: 31 KJV

## Life Changing Faith

Since faith in Jesus is the only way,
That one may God's kingdom gain,
We can easily think that it matters not,
The lifestyle on earth we maintain.

We cannot earn our way to heaven,
By doing works of good,
Indeed we will never be good enough,
Or do all the things we should.

So what difference does it make,
How we live each day?
Believe in Jesus – isn't that enough,
To keep God's wrath away?

Faith in Jesus is where we start,
But even Satan knows him for sure.
Our faith must then transform our hearts,
If our life is to forever endure.

———————

"I beseech you therefore, brethren, by the mercies of God,
that ye present your bodies a living sacrifice, holy, acceptable
unto God, *which is* your reasonable service. 2 And be not
conformed to this world: but be ye transformed by the renewing of
your mind, that ye may prove what *is* that good, and acceptable,and
perfect will of God."
Romans 12: 1 & 2 KJV

C.R. Hill, Jr.

## Life's Greatest Game

I recall a game we played,
When I was just a child.
Hide and Seek was its name,
And it could get quite wild.

It was fun to seek for one,
Who could very cleverly hide.
I remember we would search,
For that one far and wide.

Childhood days are now long passed,
Yet still life has a game to play.
It is not a game of childhood fun,
It has a greater prize to pay.

The game calls us to seek the Lord,
With all of our heart and soul,
And the prize we gain at life's end,
Is heaven's glorious goal.

———

"Seek the LORD, and his strength:
seek his face evermore."
Psalm 105: 4 KJV

"Brethren, I count not myself to have apprehended:
But *this* one thing *I do*, forgetting those things which
are behind, and reaching forth unto those things which
are before, 14 I press toward the mark for the prize of the
high calling of God in Christ Jesus."
Philippians 3: 13&14 KJV

## Life's Eternal Prize

A cross was found in the rubble,
When those Twin Towers fell.
Now alien voices want it removed,
They wish no one its story tell.

But God has acted in his love,
By that cross humankind he does save,
And those now wishing to have it gone,
Will wish they hadn't in their grave.

For God has given his decree,
On his throne he has set his Son,
That all who in faith do turn to him,
Will live on when earthly life is done.

But those who here reject his grace,
Who his very name despise,
Will in derision be cast out,
Never gaining life's eternal prize.

———————

Read Psalm 2

"Then shall he speak unto them in his wrath,
and vex them in his sore displeasure. 6 Yet have
I set my King upon my holy hill of Zion."
Psalm 2: 5 & 6 KJV

C.R. Hill, Jr.

## Like a Beacon in the Night

We were flying late one night,
Making our way home.
Many lights from towns below,
Through the darkness shown.

Yet none of these many scattered lamps,
Could help us our course complete,
None could us lead to the path,
That would put ground beneath our feet.

Then a flash lit up our plane,
As it shown in the cockpit bright.
The single circling beam it was,
Of the airport's beacon light.

O how our lives are like that night,
Traveling through this darkened world,
There are many scattered lamps that call,
That would our lives to darkness hurl.

Yet there is a beacon that flashes bright,
Its light fills our inner soul.
It is the light of Christ our Lord,
Leading to life's eternal goal.

———

"God is faithful, by whom ye were
called unto the fellowship of his
Son Jesus Christ our Lord."
1Corinthians 1: 9 KJV

## Like A Vessel At God's Side

Like a water bottle on a hiker's side,
A container for the hiker to fill,
With filtered water clean and pure,
To refresh his soul at his will.

So is the one who walks with God,
As he travels through each day.
It is God who carries him along,
Who seeks to travel in Christ's way.

No co-pilot the eternal God,
To bless and sanction the things we do.
He is the one who charts the course,
Then calls us to follow true.

As empty vessels at his side,
He fills us fresh as the day begins,
Then uses us as his path we share,
And by our use other souls he wins.

———————

"Humble yourselves therefore
under the mighty hand of God, that
he may exalt you in due time,
7 Casting all your care upon him:
for he careth for you."
1Peter 5:6 & 7 KJV.

C.R. Hill, Jr.

## Like Mountain Thunder Rolls

There is a word - a written word,
That brings to life the dead,
That word that calms the wildest storm,
Whenever in faith it's read.

That word, you ask, where is it found?
On the pages of God's book.
The story there of Jesus Christ,
Is where one needs to look.

There in reading from verse to verse,
The Lord of life is known,
As he leaps from every page,
Making the reader's heart his throne.

So take the Book and digest it well,
For God's living Word it holds,
And from each page God's saving grace,
Like mountain thunder rolls.

———————

"...these are written, that ye might believe
that Jesus is the Christ, the Son of God;
and that believing ye might have life
through his name."
John 20:31 KJV

## Lion Slayers

A lion prowls in search of prey,
The tiger stalks its quarry.
The devil seeks an unwary soul,
To fill its heart with worry.

For worry is a favorite tool,
In his arsenal of pain.
If he can fill a heart with fear,
He can in the end his victim gain.

Yet Jesus is the antidote,
To all of Satan's schemes.
By faith in him a soul is freed,
To realize God's greatest dreams.

For Jesus drives all fears away,
God's peace through grace he gives,
And he who follows him in trust,
Forever in God's kingdom lives.

---

Read John 17: 1-11 & 1Peter 5:6-11

"But the God of all grace, who hath called
us unto his eternal glory by Christ Jesus,
after that ye have suffered a while, make
you perfect, stablish, strengthen, settle *you*.
11 To him *be* glory and dominion for ever
and ever. Amen."
1Peter 5: 10 & 11 KJV

C.R. Hill, Jr.

## Live for the Long View

What will you have at the end of the day,
If not some soul who has heaven gained,
Who by your influence upon their life,
Did come to trust in Jesus' name?

A few changes here on this earth of ours,
Perhaps your influence can make,
But how soon will it all be forgotten by men,
If it no eternal difference did make?

Life at its best is but a brief span,
Most live it for what the moment will bring,
But what worth is it at the end of the day,
If for heaven you laid up not a thing.

Consider the time you have here on earth,
And the chances it affords for the long view.
Then make the time count for investing above,
And treasures in heaven will await you.

––––––––––

"And whosoever shall give to drink
unto one of these little ones a cup of cold water
only in the name of a disciple,
verily I say unto you, he shall in no wise
lose his reward."
Matthew 10: 42  KJV

## Living Water

It was from the rock the water came,
When Israel thirsted so.
It is always from the rock of God,
That his living waters flow.

We thirst today for something more,
Than things or ease can bring.
We too thirst as did those of old,
For the living rock our king.

It is Jesus Christ, who is the rock,
That will quench our soul's deep thirst,
If with heart and soul and mind and strength,
We in our living will put him first.

Then from our heart as he has said,
Living waters like a mountain spring,
Will flow down in sparkling streams,
As every drop life abundant will bring.

———

"Behold, I will stand before thee there
upon the rock in Horeb; and thou shalt
smite the rock, and there shall come water
out of it, that the people may drink. And
Moses did so in the sight of the elders of Israel."
Exodus 17: 6 KJV

C.R. Hill, Jr.

# Miracles of Grace

I saw a miracle the other day,
And I thought I'd done something right.
But God quickly gave a reminder to me,
That it was all the result of his might.

So many times we think it is us,
When good follows something we've done.
Then we swell up with a false pride,
And forget we depend on God's Son.

The truth of the matter if any good comes,
It is always the result of God's grace.
He just puts us there to watch what he does,
When we faithfully focus on his face.

So the next time it's a miracle you need,
Don't think it's depending on you.
It is Jesus who the miracles performs,
Just trust what in his grace he will do.

———————

"I am the vine, ye are the branches.
He that abideth in me, and I in him,
the same bringeth forth much fruit:
for without me ye can do nothing."
John 15: 5 KJV

## Mystifying Grace

When I look into God's word,
A mystery I often see.
I read a verse that sounds so strange,
And wonder what does it mean to me?

That Jesus is the true Son of God,
Is one that blows my mind.
Yet in him God himself has come,
Into the creation he designed.

Then there upon Golgotha's cross,
God himself assumed the blame,
For all the sins that I have done,
And of all the world's the same.

The mystery still overwhelms my mind,
How through faith I can receive,
My sins forgiven and eternal life,
Because in Jesus I do believe.

———————

"Even the mystery which hath been hid
from ages and from generations, but now
is made manifest to his saints:  27 To whom
God would make known what is the riches
of glory of this mystery among the Gentiles;
which is Christ in you, the hope of glory:"
Colossians 1: 26 & 27 KJV

C.R. Hill, Jr.

# Never Alone

"The earth is the Lord's and the fullness thereof,"
That is a fact that we most often forget.
We think it is ours and we stand alone,
As then through each day we fret.

We think we have it all to do by ourselves,
If we've any hope of staying alive.
Yet God has our back if our hope is in him,
It is his grace that lets our soul thrive.

So lift up your heart, rejoice in the news,
God has not left you alone.
Do you feel the world is against you?
The world is the footstole of God's throne.

Holy is the ground upon which you stand,
Along with everything in God's sight.
And all who in him their hope do lean,
He delivers from distress by his might.

---

"Behold, the eye of the Lord *is* upon them
that fear him, upon them that hope in his mercy;
19 To deliver their soul from death,
and to keep them alive in famine."
Psalm 33: 18 & 19 KJV

"What shall we then say to these things?
If God *be* for us, who *can be* against us?
32 He that spared not his own Son, but
delivered him up for us all, how shall he
not with him also freely give us all things?"
Romans 8:31 & 32 KJV

## Not Guilty

I am acquitted - free from every charge,
Standing in God's judgment hall.
In that eternal courtroom scene I hear,
"Not guilty! God's grace does him enthrall."

A slave am I to the grace of God,
Held spellbound before his throne.
From whence has come this marvelous gift?
Ah, it comes from Christ Jesus alone.

For guilty I before his cross,
Came with hands so stained by sin,
And there he took all of my guilt away,
Then died my salvation for to win.

It is now only by my faith in him,
I stand here from guilt set free,
Remembering that great fateful day,
When I realized Jesus had died for me.

---

"There is therefore now no condemnation
to them which are in Christ Jesus, who walk
not after the flesh, but after the Spirit."
Romans 8:1 KJV

C.R. Hill, Jr.

# O Sing of the Shepherd

Many I see in this world today,
Who are walking through life alone.
They've yet to receive the Shepherd's grace,
Or allowed him to make them his own.

Therefore, ye lambs who are carried by him,
Share without fear your good news.
Hesitate not to let it be known,
That he will carry them too if they choose.

It is only the heart that keeps one apart,
From the abundance of life Jesus gives.
If one will but yield in faith and in trust,
He will make their heart a home where he lives.

O tell of his love wherever you go;
Many hunger for the news that you bring.
The songs he gives that ring in your heart,
are given so that others can sing.

———————

"Behold, the Lord God will come with strong *hand*,
and his arm shall rule for him: behold, his reward is
with him, and his work before him. 11 He shall feed
his flock like a shepherd: he shall gather the lambs
with his arm, and carry *them* in his bosom, *and* shall
gently lead those that are with young."
Isaiah 40: 10 & 11 KJV

## Oddballs

When you live in a land where the majority rules,
It is quite easy to just follow the crowd.
Yet in such a land the oddball stands out,
And their difference often speaks very loud.

I went to Chicago when the tall ships were in,
They were moored at the Navy Pier.
Impressive were they with mast and sails,
But it's by an odd part called a rudder they steer.

So the crowd thinks it's cool to do this or that,
To live and behave certain ways.
Yet it is usually the oddball who sets the trends,
That the crowd wants to lavish with praise.

It's all up to you as you live in this land,
To decide to which one you'll adhere.
Will you just blend in and follow the crowd,
Or be the oddball, the rudder, and steer?

––––––––––

"And Jesus said unto them,
Come ye after me, and I will
make you to become fishers of men."
Mark 1: 17 KJV

"These that have turned the world upside down
are come hither also; 7 Whom Jason hath received:
and these all do contrary to the decrees of Caesar,
saying that there is another king, *one* Jesus."
Acts 17: 6b & 7 KJV

C.R. Hill, Jr.

## On An April Afternoon

I was walking late one April day,
Across an old church yard.
My life was deeply buried in sin,
My soul was badly scarred.

Great shame did my heart envelop,
Too sad was I even to cry.
Then Jesus came and spoke to me,
"For your sins my death was why."

Then by his arms of love and grace,
His Spirit lifted my sins away,
Joy filled my heart and soul,
As I received him on that April day.

Long my road has been since then,
Now over fifty years I have come,
And I have rejoiced every day,
In what Jesus for me has done.

———

"For I am not ashamed of the gospel
of Christ: for it is the power of God unto
salvation to every one that beleiveth;
to the Jew first, and also to the Greek."
Romans 1: 16 KJV

I Talked With Him This Morning

## On Parchments of Hearts

When I look upon my office wall,
And see the parchments framed and hung,
I wonder what value they will have,
When my course on earth is run?

They speak to others of what I achieved,
But they remind me of God's supply.
For none of them would I have earned,
Had I been made on myself to rely.

The only parchments when this life shall end,
That will be long remembered if at all,
Will be the parchments of the human hearts,
I may have helped rescue from the fall.

For Jesus sent me out to preach his news,
That he came from sin and death to save,
So all who here do trust in his grace,
Will forever live beyond the grave.

————

"Ye are our epistle written in our hearts,
known and read of all men:  3 Forasmuch
as ye are manifestly declared to be the epistle
of Christ ministered by us written not with ink,
but with the Spirit of the living God; not in tables
of stone, but in fleshly tables of the heart."
2Corinthians 3: 2 & 3 KJV,

C.R. Hill, Jr.

## On This Easter Day

There is a decision now to make,
To receive or not the news.
For Christ has died our souls to save,
If we will his offering choose.

"For many" does the Bible say,
He bore their sins upon the cross,
But he knew many on hearing the news,
Would choose his gift of life to toss.

So where stand you this Easter Day,
As you hear the news that he has risen?
Will you in faith receive him in,
Or reject his salvation given?

Many do for the moment concede,
And join the resurrection crowd,
Yet as the day of Easter fades,
They reject Jesus who left the shroud.

———

"...he hath poured out his soul unto death:
and he was numbered with the transgressors;
and he bare the sin of many, and made intercession
for the transgressors."
Isaiah 53: 12b KJV

"...if thou shalt confess with thy mouth
the Lord Jesus, and shalt believe in thine heart
that God hath raised him from the dead,
thou shalt be saved."
Romans 10: 9 KJV

## One Truth Tempered With Grace

There's only one truth in relation to God,
Only one Savior of all humankind.
There is no other who can do what he does,
In keeping with his eternal design.

Yet does our world demand equal time,
For expression of all of the lies.
Never mind in the end their only intent,
Is to obscure the grace God supplies.

It seems only fair that all opinions be heard,
And that we mutually respect every view.
Yet opinions aside two plus two is still four,
Nor will opinions ever change what is true.

O we must respect all those who will differ,
Even defend their right to be wrong.
And show them we must God's loving grace,
In hopes they will with God's truth come along.

———

"This [Jesus] is the stone which was set at nought
Of you builders, which is become the head of the corner.
12 Neither is there salvation in any other: for there is
none other name under heaven given among men,
whereby we must be saved."
Acts 4: 11 & 12 KJV

C.R. Hill, Jr.

## Open To Me The Gates Of Righteousness

"Winning isn't everything."
Yet many strive to win at all cost.
But what is the value of a win,
If in the contest honor is lost?

Lose the race you run today,
Then tomorrow resume the chase -
But lose your honor in the running,
And the shame a lifetime will not erase.

Our values have become askew,
If one's character now matters not.
Let integrity be the sacrifice,
And in the end what have you got?

I'd rather lose a race or two,
Or never receive the winner's crown,
Than when my earthly race is done,
Not on God's righteous team be found.

———————

"He hath shewed thee, O man, what is good;
and what doth the LORD require of thee, but
to do justly, and to love mercy, and to walk
humbly with thy God?"
Micah 6:8 KJV

"Open to me the gates of righteousness:
I will go into them, *and* I will praise the LORD:"
Psalm 118: 19 KJV

## Our Light for Heaven's Trail

Did you see the moon as Advent neared?
Did you see it light the night like noonday?
Did you see the North Star clear and bright,
As it shone to point the traveler's way?

And do you hear the voice of God,
As he is speaking through this season?
He proclaims aloud salvation's news,
The lowly manger's reason.

Hear it now as never before!
With ears of faith perceive it!
Jesus Christ has come to earth,
To make sinners here for heaven fit.

Sweetly laid in a manger rude,
Of un-planed boards and hay,
The very voice of God is robed,
In the flesh of earthly clay.

God by whom all things were made,
Has in Jesus now come to earth,
So with his blood for our sins to pay,
And give to us the second birth.

The moon, the stars we see so bright,
Do to Bethlehem's Star now pale,
As Jesus drives sin's night away,
Giving us his light for heaven's trail.

————

"All things were made by him; and
without him was not any thing made
that was made. 4 In him was life;
and the life was the light of men.
5 And the light shineth in darkness;
and the darkness comprehended it not."
John 1: 3 – 5 KJV

C.R. Hill, Jr.

## Our Rejuvenating Hope

Arise O traveler of life's toilsome way!
Take courage for your climb.
The struggle lasts but a little while,
The glory beyond all time.

Today take pause to hear God's voice;
Be still beside life's stream.
Refresh your spirit with his grace,
Then arise to seize God's dream.

The waters through which now you pass,
Are for the cleansing of your soul.
The fires are not to burn you up,
But to make you purer is their goal.

Rejoice then for what is lost is gain,
God does more than it restore.
Jesus has won an inheritance for you,
That will last forever more.

———

"And I will restore to you the years
that the locust hath eaten, the cankerworm,
and the caterpiller, and the palmerworm,
my great army which I sent among you."
Joel 2: 25 KJV

I Talked With Him This Morning

## Out of Our Strife into True Life

I find myself in a world full of folks,
Who are troubled with illness and fear.
Thinking themselves immune from strife,
They have landed as patients in here.

The disease is not the worst thing they face,
But the fear of their loss of control.
Suddenly they can't count on themselves,
To be the captain of their very own soul.

It is here that they need the news that I bring,
That they do not have to do it alone,
Indeed it is when we are too weak to hang on,
That the power of God becomes known.

It is from Jesus light has always proceeded,
In him resides all healing and life.
By his grace all of our sins are forgiven,
And by his love we're delivered from strife.

––––––––––

"Yea, though I walk through the valley
of the shadow of death, I will fear no evil:
for thou *art* with me; thy rod and thy staff
they comfort me."
Psalm 23:4 KJV

C.R. Hill, Jr.

## Passing It Along

We only share what we've been given,
By the God and Father of us all;
Without the gifts of life he gives us,
We would very quickly fall.

Yet do many walk unknowing,
Through their days of toil and care,
God surrounds their every moment,
But they have not a clue he's there.

It is then for us who by his presence,
Have been blessed beyond belief,
Although we suffer as they do,
To share his comfort that is our relief.

O may we have our eyes wide open,
To see Jesus wherever we go.
Then point him out to those in darkness,
That his comfort they also may know.

---

"Blessed be God, even the Father
of our Lord Jesus Christ, the Father
of mercies, and the God of all comfort;
4 Who comforteth us in all our tribulation,
that we may be able to comfort them which
are in any trouble, by the comfort wherewith
we ourselves are comforted of God."
2Corinthians 1: 3 & 4 KJV

## Quiet Please

I sometimes go to this quiet place,
Where I my soul by the water renew.
There just resting beneath the pines,
I enjoy the lakeside view.

There in the quiet my mind I refresh,
With little to pass the time;
Except to walk by the water's edge,
Or watch the fly on the end of my line.

It's good to escape from the rush of the day,
To a place where the heart can hear.
There in the stillness a body can rest,
And experience God's presence so near.

I sometimes wish I could always stay,
In such a place where no troubles invade,
But God bids me back into the rush,
And the folks there in need of his aid.

---

"Be still, and know that I *am* God:"
Psalm 46: 10 KJV

C.R. Hill, Jr.

## Redeem The Day

O how the time goes flying by,
From dawn to setting sun.
O how so many miss the chances,
To walk with God's only Son.

Awake O Sleeper – arise and see,
Today's the day to grace receive,
To stand among the saints redeemed,
Who in their time did in Jesus believe.

Go you heralds, proclaim the news,
While today the chance you have,
To offer to every sin-sick soul,
God's soothing - healing salve.

O use the time you have today,
To change a life or two,
To offer Jesus to the souls you meet,
So they in him may be born anew.

———————

"Wherefore he saith, 'Awake thou that sleepest,
and arise from the dead, and Christ shall give thee light.
See then that ye walk circumspectly, not as fools,
but as wise, Redeeming the time, because the days are evil."
Ephesians 5:14 – 16 KJV

I Talked With Him This Morning

## Reflections From the Wall

On the mall in blackened stone,
Engraved there are the names,
Of children who gave up their lives,
Before you were playing games.

And now reflecting like a mirror,
The image of you and me.
The wall calls out and speaks to us,
Of what they died to let us be.

Their names appear on blackened stone,
They had little choice for their giving,
Their time called them to give up their life,
That we in freedom could go on living.

So pause and muse with me the wall,
Give head those silent voices,
And guard the gifts they bought for you,
By making wise and noble choices.

———————

"For, brethren, ye have been called unto liberty;
only *use* not liberty for an occasion to the flesh,
but by love serve one another. 14 For all the law
is fulfilled in one word, *even* in this; THOU SHALT
LOVE THY NEIGHBOR AS THYSELF."
Galatians 5:13 & 14 KJV

"Greater love hath no man than this, that
a man lay down his life for his friends."
John 15:13 KJV

C.R. Hill, Jr.

## Reflections of The Father

In Christ you are a people,
Holy in God's sight.
In Christ you have been chosen,
To be a bearer of God's light.

Not because you were so special,
Above all others on the earth,
But because the Lord is faithful,
To honor his sure sworn oath.

He has promised all to Jesus,
Who do come in faith and trust,
Will be given life eternal,
Not abandoned to the dust.

Their sins will be forgiven,
Their wills and hearts be changed,
Their former ways of living,
Will be for Jesus' way exchanged.

———————

Read Deuteronomy 7: 6 -16

"For thou *art* an holy people unto the LORD
thy God: the LORD thy God hath chosen thee
to be a special people unto himself, above all
people that *are* upon the face of the earth."
Deuteronomy 7: 6 KJV

I Talked With Him This Morning

# Remember Who Your Father Is

When as a boy I would leave the house,
My mother would call out and say,
"Remember who your father is!"
I can still her voice today.

It was her way of reminding me,
That no matter where I went,
My actions would reflect on him,
Oh I knew exactly what she meant.

Those words ring out still loud and clear,
Among her lessons they are the best,
They remind me now that who I am,
Does on my faith in Jesus rest.

Through the cleansing he has wrought,
He made my life holy to become,
A dwelling place for our Father God,
That makes me of course a son.

———————

Read Romans 8: 1 - 17

"For as many as are led by the Spirit of God,
they are the sons of God.  15 For ye have not
received the spirit of bondage again to fear;
but ye have received the Spirit of adoption,
whereby we cry, Abba Father."
Romans 8: 14 & 15 KJV

C.R. Hill, Jr.

# Security!

"Security!" that is the word in vogue today.
At every turn there is the camera's eye.
Yet most disregard the watchful view,
Of the Lord who reigns on high.

Security –the thing we crave to have!
Let us feel safe wherever we are,
In our world that is anything but safe,
We want danger kept from us far.

We place our trust in bank accounts,
We put alarms and cameras in our home,
We rely on guns and guards,
To protect us from every evil known.

While Jesus watches the ways of men,
As he reigns from heaven's throne,
And holds those secure in his hand,
Who on his grace their trust have thrown.

---

Read Psalm 33: 13-22

"Behold, the eye of the Lord
*is* upon them that fear him,
upon them that hope in his mercy;
19 To deliver their soul from death,
and to keep them alive in famine."
Psalm 33: 18 & 19 KJV

I Talked With Him This Morning

## Springs In The Hard Places

How many times have I felt hemmed in?
Between a rock and a hard place I have said,
My hope seemed gone, my spirit weak,
I thought I was as good as dead!

"Why, O God, have you brought me here?"
In despair to the heavens I have cried!
"Why not leave me in that other place,
Where in comfort I could have died?"

Yet it has been in life's desert dry,
That God has shown me best his hand.
When between hard place and rock I'm pinned,
Where I can only on God's promise stand.

It is then the hard place becomes a spring,
And the rock becomes a lavish pool.
Then it is my soul rejoices in God,
As in his renewing grace I cool.

———

"Tremble, thou earth, at the presence of the Lord, at the
presence of the God of Jacob; 8 Which turned the rock
*into* a standing water, the flint into a fountain of waters."
Psalm 114: 7 & 8 KJV

## C.R. Hill, Jr.

## Standing on the Promises

I saw the storm on the distant hills,
I heard its approaching thunder roll,
I began to quake –then I heard God say,
"Fear not! It is still under my control.

I will shelter you within my grace,
Though the storm about you roar,
You shall hear, and see, and feel its rage,
Yet my protection it can't ignore.

And when the winds are still again,
When the clouds have cleared the sky,
All who look upon your life,
Will see I your prayers did not deny.

For I am the Lord of all that is,
I have created you to be my own.
I will never forsake a single soul,
To whom I've made my promise known."

---

"Rest in the LORD, and wait patiently for him:
fret not thyself because of him who prospereth
in his way, because of the man who bringeth
wicked devices to pass."
Psalm 37:7 KJV

## Starting From Nothing

How many times have I held in my hand,
Something that I thought worth nothing at all?
Then later discovered for it a great use;
It has happened more often than I can recall.

Now if I a man can make something of nothing,
Imagine what can happen in God's hands.
When we give him ourselves as small as we feel,
He can make a life that eternity spans.

How many times have I heard his voice call,
And I've thought I had nothing to give.
Yet at his command I've gone to the task,
And a something from nothing did live.

I am sure that like me you too often feel,
That you are not up to doing what God asks.
Just take what you have and entrust it to him,
And he will use it to accomplish his task.

———————

Read Matthew 14: 13-21

"But Jesus said unto them, They need not depart;
give ye them to eat. 17 And they say unto him,
We have here but five loaves, and two fishes.
18 He said, Bring them hither to me."
Matthew 14: 16-18 KJV

C.R. Hill, Jr.

## Still Singing through the Sorrow

Who can laugh when times are hard,
Or be glad though sufferings come?
The one who has found peace with God,
By trusting God's dear Son.

They through weary days of pain,
Still wear upon their face a smile,
And though the body may weaker grow,
Their spirit grows stronger all the while.

They tread the upward paths of sorrow,
Yea, even tearful grow at times,
Yet breathlessly they still press on,
Knowing thus God their gold refines.

So take courage friends if pain you know,
And in your hard times still rejoice,
For Jesus suffered even death for you,
So life eternal could be your choice.

---

"And not only *so*, but we glory in tribulations also:
knowing that tribulation worketh patience; 4 And
patience, experience; and experience, hope: 5 And
hope maketh not ashamed; because the love of God
is shed abroad in our hearts by the Holy Ghost which
is given unto us."
Romans 5: 3-5 KJV

## Such As You Have

Do you have it to give away,
Those words that can a life change?
They spring forth from a heart of faith,
And another's heart can rearrange.

So many whom we see today,
Are so crippled by life's strain,
They sit immobile by life's busy gate,
Begging for anything to ease their pain.

Yet what they need by silver or gold,
Can never their answer secure.
Jesus alone whose life-changing grace,
Will transform their life with his cure.

Yet that transformation is waiting for one,
Who in Jesus with total confidence,
Will utter the words with no doubt in their heart,
That will make in those lives the difference.

———————

"Then Peter said, Silver and gold have I none;
but such as I have give I thee: In the name of
Jesus Christ of Nazareth rise up and walk."
Acts 3:6 KJV

"Hear him, ye deaf; His praise, ye dumb,
Your loosened tongues employ;
Ye blind, behold your Savior come;
And leap, ye lame, for joy." *

*From the hymn "O For A Thousand Tongues"
by Charles Wesley

C.R. Hill, Jr.

# Summons To Witness

Saul was kicking and screaming,
But was given no choice,
When a light from heaven came,
And he heard Jesus' voice.

He was sent into the city,
There he was told what to do.
Perhaps not as dramatic,
Is God's calling to you.

Nonetheless, to you God is calling,
Though you be kicking and screaming.
Our God is enlisting disciples,
As he is his creation redeeming.

Yet you have a choice,
Accept God's assignment,
Or sit on his grace –
keeping his light in confinement.

————

Read Acts 9: 1-9

"And he said, Who art thou, Lord?  And the Lord said,
I am Jesus whom thou persecutest: *it is* hard for thee to
kick against the pricks.  6 And he trembling and astonished
said, Lord, what wilt thou have me to do?  And the Lord
*said* unto him, Arise, and go into the city, and it shall be
told thee what thou must do."
Acts 9: 5 & 6 KJV

## Surrender?

A rich young man to Jesus came,
God's kingdom he wished to claim.
But when Jesus told him to sell his goods,
He thought by too high a price it came.

O we may not think ourselves so rich,
In the earthly wealth we hold,
But even pennies in our pocket change,
Can become as heavy as bars of gold.

It all depends on what we do,
When God says, "Give it up and follow me."
Can we bring ourselves to give it away,
So the kingdom's gates we may see?

The smallest treasure can be so large,
That it can completely block our sight.
The largest treasure is far too small,
To be worth our missing heaven's delight.

———

"Now when Jesus heard these things,
he said unto him, Yet lackest thou one thing:
sell all that thou hast, and distribute unto the poor,
and thou shalt have treasure in heaven; and come,
follow me. And when he heard this, he was
very sorrowful: for he was very rich."
Luke 18: 22 & 23 KJV

C.R. Hill, Jr.

# Temples of the Lord

God seeks a place to dwell in,
Among the creation he has formed,
For the rebellion of his enemy,
Has his earthly temple scorned.

The people he had fashioned,
In his holy image true,
Chose to disobey him,
Then his presence hardly knew.

So he formed a special nation,
Surely they would seek his face.
He designed for them his temple,
But they just cluttered up his place.

Then he turned at last to Jesus,
Sent him to earth to die for sin.
Now all who do in him believe,
Are the holy temple he dwells in.

———————

"Know ye not that ye are the temple of God,
and *that* the Spirit of God dwelleth in you?
17 If any man defile the temple of God,
him shall God destroy; for the temple
of God is holy, which *temple* ye are."
1Corinthians 3:16 & 17 KJV

I Talked With Him This Morning

## The Leader of My Soul

When I set the Lord before me,
Always as my guide,
Then I walk with steady steps,
As I seek to match his stride.

My heart is glad along the way,
In fellowship with him;
Joy fills me through and through,
With his life that has no end.

I lie down at night and rise at dawn,
Secure with Christ am I,
For his presence shields my soul,
From all that would my life deny.

So I'll walk on from day to day,
Through whatever life may bring,
And when my trail has ended here,
I will then in heaven sing.

---

"For thou hast delivered my soul from death,
mine eyes from tears, *and* my feet from falling.
9 I will walk before the Lord in the land of the living."
Psalm 116: 8 & 9 KJV

C.R. Hill, Jr.

# The Calling

I am often blinded by my desires,
And fail to see God's plan.
I willfully go along my way,
And ignore his guiding hand.

O let me, Lord, today be yours,
Help me your word to heed,
May I be faithful to your voice,
And your every directive heed.

Give me a heart that really cares,
And a love for all I meet.
Then when today my work is done,
May it be an offering laid at your feet.

Teach me Jesus your work to do,
The way you'd have it done,
And when the day is finished here,
May a soul for heaven been won.

―――――――

Read Acts 9:1-19

"…Arise, and go into the city, and it
shall be told thee what thou must do."
Acts 9: 6b KJV

## The Challenge of the Upside Down

I've been looking at the world all wrong,
I've been seeing it all upside down.
I've been looking at things in time,
Hoping faith would turn them around.

I see now my need for the longer view,
That it is for God's kingdom I must strive.
Then use the temporal things as they come,
As the tools to help that goal arrive.

This idea is too strange to me,
Like trying to stand upon my head all day.
Yet the thought is so intriguing and new,
I am going to try it anyway.

I'll start by asking this pointed question,
When with a temporal challenge I'm faced,
"What is the eternal lesson for me,
About God's kingdom goal I chase?"

---

"…not only *so,* but we glory in tribulations also;
knowing that tribulation worketh patience;
4 And patience, experience; and experience, hope:
5 And hope maketh not ashamed; because the love of God
is shed abroad in our hearts by the Holy Ghost
which is given unto us."
Romans 5:3 – 5 KJV

C.R. Hill, Jr.

# The Climbs That Shape the Soul

There are days when the path is steep,
And the load so hard to bear.
Then temptations raise their heads,
Crying, "Why not quit! Why even care?

Why not leave your chosen trail,
Of following the Lord's footprints,
Why not go where the masses walk,
It seems to make more sense?"

Yet in my heart of hearts I know,
That the steep climbs shape the soul,
The heavy loads we carry there,
Are what it takes to reach God's goal.

So I'll strengthen my weak knees,
I'll lift up my drooping hands,
Then find the straight path for my feet,
To that peak where Jesus stands.

---

"Wherefore lift up the hands which hang down,
and the feeble knees; 13 And make straight paths
for your feet, lest that which is lame be turned
out of the way; but let it rather be healed."
Hebrews 12: 12 & 13 KJV

## The Confession of A Desert Rat

In the deserts of our own design,
We wander on as strength grows weak
All the while we ignore the Rock,
Where springs the waters that we seek.

It is bread we crave that can satisfy,
The deepest hungers of our soul!
But refuse its offer if its source,
Is something other than we control.

We perish upon such desert waste,
Rejecting the grace God offers free,
We drink the dust from our empty wells,
As we refuse God's offered  grace to see.

When will our stubborn hearts wake up,
And turn to see God's fruited plain?
When will we flee our self-made ways
Then return to God and heaven gain?

————

"Wherefore do ye spend money
for that which is not bread?
And your labour for that which satisfieth not?
Hearken diligently unto me, and eat ye
that which is good, and let your soul delight
itself in fatness.  Incline your ear, and come unto me:
hear, and your soul shall live;…"
Isaiah 55: 2 – 3a KJV

C.R. Hill, Jr.

## The Cornerstone

O how lost is the world I see,
With no faith in Christ my Lord.
They walk through life without a clue,
About God's redeeming Word.

It is not just a word upon a page,
Or one springing from the tongue,
It is God's eternal living Word,
Expressed in Jesus Christ his Son.

God's living Word did flesh assume,
To become just as human here as we,
Then took upon himself our sins,
And paid for them on Calvary.

God's Living Stone he has become,
By whom lives or dies each soul.
In disbelief reject him and die,
Or trust him for life eternal's goal.

———————

"Unto you therefore which believe he is precious:
but unto them which be disobedient, the stone
which the builders disallowed, the same is made
the head of the corner, 8 And a stone of stumbling,
and a rock of offence, *even to them* which stumble
at the word, being disobedient: whereunto also
they were appointed."
1Peter 2:7 & 8 KJV

## The Country Next Door

There is a country not too far,
In fact it is right next door.
Of those who venture there,
Few are heard from anymore.

Its citizens are more about having fun,
A good time is all that they seek,
Of building lives that a difference make,
You will seldom hear them speak.

By first name only they are mostly known,
No tracing their roots or kin,
No name that will be remembered long,
When their life on earth shall end.

There are but few, who by God's grace,
When in that land themselves they find,
Awaken from its delusional sleep,
And return to the life that God designed.

———

"And when he came to himself, he said, How many hired
servants of my father's have bread enough and to spare,
and I perish with hunger! 18 I will arise and go to my father,
and will say unto him, Father, I have sinned against heaven,
and before thee, 19 And am no more worthy to be called thy son: make
me as one of thy hired servants....24 For this my son
was dead, and is alive again; he was lost, and is found.
And they began to be merry."
Luke 15: 17-19 & 24 KJV

C.R. Hill, Jr.

## The Covering of God's Grace

I read God's Word and realize I'm undone,
For his laws and commands I've broken.
He has made it clear what his will demands,
In all that he has spoken.

While I desire to live steadfast and true,
I find his demands impossible to meet,
It is then I fall in failure's tears,
At my Savior Jesus' feet.

For all I find that I could not do,
Though it was my heart's sincere desire,
Jesus has done on my behalf,
Saving me from hell's eternal fire.

He has clothed me in his righteousness,
Given me a status I could never achieve,
Asking only that I in return will trust,
As I in his great salvation believe.

———

"O that my ways were directed
to keep thy statutes!"
Psalm 119:5 KJV

"Think not that I am come to destroy the law,
or the prophets: I am not come to destroy, but to fulfill,"
Matthew 5:17 KJV

## The Doorkeeper's Watch

"You my child have been appointed,
To stand by the door and watch;
Then take the hands of searching souls,
And place them upon the latch.

Keep one ear tuned to the music inside,
And the other to cries of the lost.
Cry back to them, 'The door is here,
Where Jesus has paid the full cost.'

Then reach for their hand,
And guide it with love,
Until the latch they hold in their palm,
And they enter into life from above.

Stay on and watch, lest they turn in fear,
And seek to exit once more.
Then when the time comes I'll say to you,
'Come on in, while a brother watches the door.'"

———

"Enter ye in at the strait gate; for wide is the gate,
and broad is the way, that leadeth to destruction,
and many there be which go in thereat:
Because strait is the gate, and narrow is the way,
which leadeth unto life, and few there be that find it."
Matthew 7: 13 & 14 KJV

C.R. Hill, Jr.

## The Empty-Handed Servant

With empty hands and empty heart,
I sit and wait today,
I have no power or desire,
To continue in God's way.

Yet neither is there the will to flee,
Or to seek different avenue.
I simply sit and wait for God,
To my spirit make anew.

It is the empty-handed soul,
That God with effect can use,
To reach a power hungry world,
With his great salvation's news.

When I think that I have the gifts,
I the gospel news impede,
It is when I fully powerless feel,
God's word gains its greatest speed.

———————

"But God hath chosen the foolish things of the world
to confound the wise; and God hath chosen
the weak things of the world to confound
the things which are mighty; 28 And base things
of the world, and things which are despised,
hath God chosen, yea, and things which are not,
to bring to nought things that are:
1Corinthians 1:27 & 28 KJV

## The Enduring Disciple

Build your life upon Jesus,
And you'll build a life that is true,
But only if every morning,
You start out with him anew.

To follow Jesus is a decision one makes,
It is a life defining set of the soul,
But it is one that one must renew every day,
If in the end they are to reach their goal.

Some days you will be staring,
From some mountaintop into the distance,
Some days you'll be facing steep climbs,
That present overwhelming resistance.

Yet it is the life that stays with him,
Enduring whatever each day may bring,
Defined by the decision to follow,
That in the end of God's victory will sing.

---

"…but he that endureth to the end shall be saved."
Matthew 10: 22b KJV

"…but *this* one thing *I do*, forgetting those
things which are behind, and reaching forth
unto those things which are before, 14 I press
toward the mark for the prize of the high calling
of God in Christ Jesus."
Philippians 3: 13b &14 KJV

"Wherefore, seeing we also are compassed about
with so great a cloud of witnesses, let us lay  aside
every weight, and the sin which doth so easily beset *us*,
and let us run with patience the race that is set before us,
2 Looking unto Jesus the author and finisher of *our* faith;…."
Hebrews 12: 1 &2a KJV

C.R. Hill, Jr.

## The Father's Dependents

Every creature that moves on the earth,
Looks to God's gifting hand.
Every creature on earth that is except,
The one made in God's image – man.

The rest know they are dependent on God,
They never question the fact at all.
One would think the most intelligent one,
Surely on God for his needs would call.

Yet this two-legged creature so full of talk,
Tends to think he has it figured out,
Pride is the reason for his "I'll do it myself."
He'd rather die than to God give a shout.

But God just patiently waits for him,
To be in a place with a wall at his back,
Then fall on his knees and lift up a prayer,
Admitting he too is depending on God to act.

———————

"O LORD, how manifold are thy works! In wisdom hast thou made them all: the earth is full of thy riches. 25 *So is* this great and wide sea, wherein *are* things creeping innumerable, both small and great beasts. 26 There go the ships: *there* is that leviathan, *whom* thou hast made to play therein. 27 These wait all upon thee; that thou mayest give *them* their meat in due season. 28 *That* thou givest them they gather: thou openest thine hand, they are filled with good."
Psalm 104: 24-28 KJV

## The Final Hour's Chime

From whence my friend, do you draw life,
From where does your meaning come?
Do you thrive on the things of time,
Or derive your life from God's own Son?

It is a choice God gives to you,
To decide which course you'll take.
Choose the way that the flesh prescribes,
Or for the Spirit's path your choice make.

When Jesus rose and to heaven went,
He sent his Spirit to take his place,
And those who chose to follow him,
Will at this life's end behold his face.

But those who chose by the flesh to live,
Taking the path of the things of time,
Will have received their full reward,
At their final hour's chime.

———

"Therefore let all the house of Israel know assuredly,
that God hath made that same Jesus, whom ye have crucified,
both Lord and Christ. 37 Now when they heard *this*, they were pricked
in their heart, and said unto Peter and the rest of the apostles, Men *and*
brethren, what shall we do? 38 Then Peter said unto them, Repent, and
be baptized every one of you in the name of Jesus Christ for the
remission of sins, and ye shall receive the gift of the Holy Ghost."
Acts 2:36 – 39 KJV

C.R. Hill, Jr.

## The Gate of the Lord

A gate I spy in yonder wall,
That marks the bounds of time,
The gate is small but inviting all,
Who will in faith to it resign.

The gate you ask, "What is its shape?"
It is a man with nail-prierced hands,
His name of course is Jesus Christ,
Whose grace all of heaven spans.

By faith we sinners dare to hope,
That through him our souls may pass,
And thus be blameless in God's sight,
For his life that will forever last.

O ye builders here on earth,
Who do on other ways insist,
Repent and seek this one true gate,
Lest your chance for life be missed.

———

"This gate of the Lord, into which the righteous
shall enter…22 The stone *which* the builders
refused is become the head *stone* of the corner."
Psalm 118:20 & 22 KJV

"Then said Jesus unto them again, Verily, verily,
I say unto you, I am the door of the sheep. 8 All that
ever came before me are thieves and robbers: but the sheep
did not hear them. 9 I am the door: by me if any man
enter in, he shall be saved, and shall go in and out,
and find pasture."
John 10: 7-9 KJV

## The Hand That Overcomes

Clouds of trouble engulf my path,
Thick fogs my way obscure,
Pain and sorrow all around me,
How now shall my faith endure?

"My child you only need to see,
Where next a step to make,
For though the path you cannot see,
Fear not for you my hand did take.

Neither rocks nor roots nor unseen pearl,
Will cause my child to fall,
No climb so steep, or cavern deep,
Can defeat those who on me call.

My path is not an easy path,
It is a narrow and toilsome climb.
Yet all who take their cross in faith,
My eternal life will find."

———————

Read Romans 8: 31-39

"Who shall separate us from the love of Christ?...
38a For I am persuaded, that [nothing]...39b shall be
able to separate us form the love of God, which is in
Christ Jesus our Lord."
Romans 8: 35a, 38a, & 39b KJV

C.R. Hill, Jr.

## The Helmsman My God

I found myself in a wilderness,
Where need did me overwhelm.
There my trust in God grew faint,
So I put myself at the helm.

I felt it was what I had to do,
I saw no help from up above.
There in a desert no water in sight,
I forgot to rely on God's love.

Quickly the passion I had for my Lord,
Began each day bit by bit to wane;
Until in this moment I am reminded anew,
I must depend on God to send the rain.

I'll give up the helm - give it over to God!
I will trust and obey his commands.
Then daily I'll pause to look at my life,
Giving thanks that I am still in God's hands.

———

Read Exodus 16: 1-30

"Then said the LORD unto Moses, Behold,
I will rain bread from heaven for you; and the
people shall go out and gather a certain rate
every day, that I may prove them, whether they
will walk in my law, or no."
Exodus 16: 4 KJV

I Talked With Him This Morning

## The Honored Seats Deserved

I read again of those in Christ,
Who great aspired to be,
Are they whose lives resemble his,
In true humility.

The great in Jesus so often are,
The last whom we'd expect,
Who before the throne of God,
Will be standing most erect.

In pride we tend to think that we,
Are the favored ones, you know,
We always strive to do things right,
So our righteousness will show.

While those humble hearts of Christ,
Who in shadows simply serve,
Will in that day before God's throne,
The honored seats deserve.

———————

Read Mark 10: 35-45

"But Jesus called them *to him*, and saith unto them,
Ye know that they which are accounted to rule
over the Gentiles exercise lordship over them;
and their great ones exercise authority upon them.
But so shall it not be among you: but whosoever
will be great among you, shall be your minister:
and whosoever of you will be the chiefest,
shall be servant of all."
Mark 10: 42 – 44 KJV

C.R. Hill, Jr.

## The Hope For A Bankrupt Soul

As a fully bankrupt soul,
I stand before God's eyes.
There are no deeds of good I have,
That can gain me the heavenly prize.

No boast at all, no work I've done,
No kindness I may have shown,
That can wash away my sinfulness,
Or make eternal life my own.

My hope depends on Jesus Christ,
And the victory he has won,
He alone conquers sin and death,
For he alone is God's Own Son.

It is only as he dwells in me,
If by full surrender I'll let him in,
That I'll have cause to hope at all,
Of gaining heaven in the end.

––––––––––

"If thou, LORD, shouldest mark iniquities,
O Lord, who shall stand? 4 But *there is*
forgiveness with thee, that thou mayest
be feared.."
Psalm 130: 3 & 4 KJV

"*Even* the mystery which hath been hid from ages
and from generations, but now is made manifest to his saints:
27 To whom God would make known what *is* the riches of the
glory of this mystery among the Gentiles; which is
Christ in you, the hope of glory:"
Colossians 1: 26 & 27 KJV

"For by grace are ye saved through faith; and
that not of yourselves: *it is* the gift of God:"
Ephesians 2: 8 KJV

129

## The Inclination of the Heart

What is the thing that defines the way,
We live out our course in life?
It is really not the hand we are dealt,
Either one of calm or strife.

It deeper goes than the surface state,
That determines the way we play our part,
We are guided in all the things we do,
By the inclination of our heart.

Yet our heart is really not a thing,
Over which we have control,
For selfish gain and sinful pride,
From birth does rule our soul.

Only God can reset the heart,
Or its inclination rearrange,
Yet when one truly hungers for it,
He will our heart's inclination change.

―――――――

"Incline my heart unto thy testimonies,
and not to covetousness."
Psalm 119: 36 KJV

"But this *shall* be the covenant that I will make
with the house of Israel; After those days saith the LORD,
I will put my law in their inward parts, and write it in their
hearts; and will be their God, and they shall be my people."
Jeremiah 31:33 KJV

C.R. Hill, Jr.

## The Inner War

There is an image I have of me,
I protect it with my pride,
But it's not the image God has for me,
To become like Jesus all inside.

I find within my heart a pull,
A tug of war between these two!
Jesus calling me to become like him,
Me not really wanting to.

O like Jesus I long to be!
Yet to do so I must of myself let go.
That's the problem that I face,
The thing with which I struggle so.

O Jesus help me to this battle lose,
That your will for me can win,
Help me to of myself let go,
That like you I may become within.

---

Read 1Kings 18, Romans 7: 21 – 25,
And Luke 9: 23 & 24

"Let this mind be in you which was also in Christ Jesus: 6 Who, being in the form of God, thought it not robbery to be equal with God: 7 But made himself of no reputation, and took upon him the form of a servant, and was made in the likeness of men: 8 And being found in fashion as a man, he humbled himself, and became obedient unto death, even the death of the cross. 9 Wherefore God also hath highly exalted him, and given him a name which is above every name: 10 That at the name of Jesus every knee should bow, of things in heaven, and things in earth, and things under the earth; 11 And that every tongue should confess that Jesus Christ is Lord, to the glory of God the Father."
Philippians 2: 5 -11 KJV

## The Light of A Faithful Shadow

I like to think of myself as a upright man,
Doing right and showing mercy, and grace.
But then I encounter that undeserving guy,
Who for my kindness would spit in my face.

Now there's a challenge hard to accept,
That to him I must continue to be kind.
Then I hear Jesus from the cross forgive,
And I have no choice but to mind.

I find it no easier that Jesus did it first,
Indeed I find it quite hard to obey.
Yet God's presence lights this path I chose,
By striving to faithfully live by his way.

I'll likely not know on this side of the grave,
What life may have been changed by my grace,
For the shadow I cast goes where I never can,
Where it may the sickness of a soul erase.

————

"Unto the upright there ariseth light in the darkness:
he is gracious, and full of compassion, and righteous."
Psalm 112:4 KJV

"And if any man will sue thee at law, and take
away thy coat, let him have *thy* cloak also."
Matthew 5: 40 KJV

C.R. Hill, Jr.

# The Meeting

Their meeting late on a moonlit night,
Beneath the ancient olive trees,
The question raised by the Lord of Life,
"Who is it that your faith sees?"

In silence he then awaited response,
As his younger brother thought.
"I guess that I have always known,
But against it I have fought."

"And now my brother, fighting still?
Or does to faith your will concede?"
"Now I believe, yet fearfully though,
For they will take your life indeed."

"Be not afraid O brother mine,
Go forth and live God's dream;
Not even death can quench your light,
When God in me you've seen."

---

"Therefore being justified by faith, we have peace
with God through our Lord Jesus Christ: 2 By
whom also we have access by faith into this grace
wherein we stand, and rejoice in hope of the glory of God.
3 And not only *so*, but we glory in tribulations also:
knowing that tribulation worketh patience; 4 And patience,
experience; and experience, hope: 5 And hope maketh not
ashamed; because the love of God is shed abroad in our hearts
by the Holy Ghost which is given unto us. "
Romans 5: 1-5 KJV

## The Light That Calms Life's Storms

So many times along my path,
I see others in such need.
I know that there is grace for them,
If they the Word of God would heed.

I also know that storms upon their sea,
Do often drown that still small voice,
In which God speaks to them,
Leaving doubts and fears their only choice.

Enter we who God's love do know,
We have seen him calm life's storms,
We know of his abundant grace,
That our every foe disarms.

Shall we keep our tongue from speaking,
Or let the light we have not show?
Shall we not share the news we have,
So those we meet can surely know?

---

"[God is the one] Which stilleth the noise
of the seas, the noise of their waves, and the
tumult of the people."
Psalm 65: 7 KJV

"But ye *are* a chosen generation, a royal priesthood,
an holy nation, a peculiar people; that ye should shew
forth the praises of him who hath called you out of
darkness into his marvellous light."
1Peter 2: 9 KJV

C.R. Hill, Jr.

# The Needle in the Straw

As a golden needle in a bale of straw,
So God's Kingdom seems to be,
This treasure of immortal worth,
Can be very hard for us to see.

Our eyes grow dull from looking,
Through life's common straws,
Our minds get full of worries,
That our daily struggles cause.

Yet hidden right before us,
Not even a fingertip away,
God's gift of life eternal,
Awaits our discovery every day.

Yea, and when by grace we see it,
When we grasp it with our mind,
Our hearts are overjoyed,
By the priceless heavenly find.

———

"Again, the kingdom of heaven is like unto
treasure hid in a field; the which when a man
hath found, he hideth, and for joy thereof goeth
and selleth all that he hath, and buyeth that field."
Matthew 13:44 KJV

135

## The Only Way

God is always searching for a soul,
To stand before him in the breach,
Between the truth of his way to life,
And the lies the pluralists teach.

It's fashionable in this world of ours,
To allow for many views,
And to think that it matters not,
Which one a soul may choose.

Yet the truth from heaven set down,
Is the road to life is only one.
That is the way that God has made,
Through Jesus Christ his Only Son.

Now many will choose to argue this,
And they never will believe,
That God himself is in Jesus Christ,
To give life to all who him receive.

———————

"Then said Jesus unto them again, Verily, verily,
I say unto you, I am the door of the sheep…..9 I am
the door: by me if any man enter in, he shall be saved,
and shall go in and out, and find pasture. 10 The thief cometh
not, but for to steal, and to kill, and to destroy: I am come that
they might have life, and that they might have *it* more abundantly."
John 10: 7 & 9 – 10 KJV

"Jesus saith unto him [Thomas], I am the way, the truth,
and the life: no man cometh unto the Father, but by me."
John 14::6 KJV

C.R. Hill, Jr.

## The Other Thief

The saddest thing I think I know,
The thing that causes me most grief,
Is the fact that in this world,
There are many like that other thief.

The one repented on the cross,
And that day to heaven with Jesus went.
The other only hung beside the Christ,
Who to save him had been sent.

He rejected God's offered grace,
When he had the chance,
He died instead in Satan's grip,
And did not beyond the grave advance.

Now all are like that other thief,
If Jesus' offer they refuse,
So trust yourself to his offered grace,
Before like the other thief you lose.

———

"Jesus saith unto him [Thomas], I am the way, the truth,
and the life: no man cometh unto the Father, but by me."
John 14: 6 KJV

"He that overcometh shall inherit all things;
and I will be his God, and he shall be my son.
8 But the fearful, and unbelieving, and the abominable,
and murderers, and whoremongers, and sorcerers,
and idolaters, and all liars, shall have their part in the lake
which burneth with fire and brimstone: which is the second death."
Revelation 21: 7 & 8 KJV

## The Path of The Spirit

The path of the Spirit,
Is for life the broad way,
Through its gateway narrow,
It leads to eternal day.

The pathway of the flesh,
Through a wide gate is found,
But it gets so narrow,
Its travelers can't turn around.

Now the pathway of the Spirit,
Through Jesus one gains,
Its fruits are the trail markers,
That one's wandering restrains.

All who follow Jesus the Lord,
Like him have the flesh crucified,
They have entered by the narrow gate,
And on God's Broadway have arrived.

---

"[The LORD] ...hast not shut me up into the hand of
the enemy: thou hast set my feet in a large room."
Psalm 31: 8 KJV

"*This* I say then, Walk in the Sprit, and ye
shall not fulfil the lust of the flesh.  22...the
fruit of the Spirit is love, joy, peace, long suffering,
gentleness, goodness, faith, 23 Meekness, temperance:
against such there is no law."
Galatians 5:16 & 22-24, KJV

C.R. Hill, Jr.

## The Path That to His Table Leads

I have a GPS, it is mounted in my car,
Its maps often look like a spaghetti bowl,
With roads going everywhere.
So it is in life with paths vying for our soul.

It often seems that any road will do,
For each one is going somewhere.
In fact so connected they seem to be,
That any one should someday get you there.

Connected be the pathways for the soul,
And in the end each does to the same place lead.
But for the journey of our soul,
These lead not to where souls on Jesus feed.

God's manna - the eternal bread of life,
Is Jesus who came to seek and save we lost.
And the only road that to his table leads,
He opened with his death on the cross.

---

"This is my beloved Son, in whom
I am well pleased; hear ye him."
Matthew 17:5b KJV

"And Jesus said unto them, I am the bread of life:
he that cometh to me shall never hunger; and he
that believeth on me shall never thirst."
John 6: 35 KJV

## The Path with the Price

I walked around looking for praise,
From people for all the good that I do.
But none of that matters at all to God,
Who only ask that to him I be true.

In fact when it is to God I am true,
People likely won't want it one bit.
To his truth they just don't want to face up,
While songs of his love seem seldom a hit.

The path that he made for saving our souls,
Runs contrary to the paths made by men.
There is no logic at all to appeal to our minds,
Like there is in the pathways of sin.

Nevertheless, for souls being redeemed,
His words are beauty, and life, and peace.
And at the end of his path in Jesus The Lord,
Is a life of glory that never shall cease.

---

"For whether *is* greater, he that sitteth at meat,
or he that serveth?  *is* not he that sitteth at meat?
But I am among you as he that serveth."
Luke 22:27 KJV

C.R. Hill, Jr.

## The Rebellion of Fools

I see a rebellion growing each day,
Among leaders and people the same.
They want to cast off all the Lord's rule,
And live with no regard for his name.

An echo I hear in the canyons of time,
Of laughter that comes from on high.
Men of all ages have played at this game,
And those kingdoms and nations did die.

It is folly to think that one can ignore,
The Creator of all things and all time,
Neither one, or a nation can last very long,
Going against the Creator's design.

It is time to repent all you dissident souls,
Of your insistence of living your way!
Turn to the Lord with sorrow in your heart,
Getting down on your knees as you pray.

———

Read Psalm 2

"Why do the heathen rage, and the people
imagine a vain thing?...4 He that sitteth in
the heavens shall laugh: the Lord shall have
them in derision....10 Be wise now therefore,
O ye kings: be instructed, ye judges of the earth.
11 Serve the LORD with fear, and rejoice with trembling.
12 Kiss the Son, lest he be angry, and ye perish *from*
the way, when his wrath is kindled but a little.
Blessed *are* all they that put their trust in him."
Psalm 2: 1 & 4 & 10-12 KJV

## The Runner

Heavy are the things I love,
The things of earthly gain.
They weight me down on my race,
And all my endurance drain.

O to leave them all behind,
To release this load I bear,
Yet they cling so closely by,
Until from God my heart they tear.

I hear the distant cheering crowd,
Those who the faithful race have run,
They call to me with hopeful cries,
To stay focused on God's Son.

O Jesus help me drop the weights,
Help me find the will to run your race,
Help me the course to finish true,
And become a victor by your grace.

———

Read Hebrews 11:32 – 12: 2.

"Wherefore, seeing we also are compassed
about with so great a cloud of witnesses,
let us lay aside every weight, and the sin
which doth so easily beset *us,* and let us
run with patience the race that is set before
us,  2 Looking unto Jesus the author and
finisher of *our* faith…."
Hebrews 12: 1& 2a KJV,

C.R. Hill, Jr.

## The Satisfied Heart

I look around on my mountain of needs,
All the things I think I must get.
But my Father says, "Forget about that,
Over the things of this life don't you fret."

"I've got plans that are different for you.
I plan to use you to refresh thirsty souls.
Be content that you are a cup in my hand,
Helping others to reach their life's goals.

So many there are who just can't understand
What it means to be a tool in my hand.
They go through life in a fretful stew,
Trying to cover every base that they can.

But those who lean on my endless supply,
Of the grace that covers their need,
End every day with a satisfied heart,
And in their prayers for more never plead."

———

"But godliness with contentment is great gain.
8 ...having food and raiment let us be therewith content.
9 ...they that will be rich fall into temptation and a snare,
and into many foolish and hurtful lusts, which drown men
in destruction and perdition... 11 But thou, O man of God,
flee these things; and follow after righteousness, godliness,
faith, love, patience, meekness."
Selected verses from
1Timothy 6: 6 -11 KJV

## The Searching Shepherd

Lost I was,
Drifted away from the Shepherd's fold.
Scattered along life's sinful ways,
Into darkness I had been sold!

Yet the Shepherd searched for me;
I heard his voice calling far away.
Would I gladly return to him,
Or turn and run the other way?

Mine was the choice to respond,
Accept his grace, or remain in sin.
I now rejoice in the day,
That I returned to him.

Still he searches every day,
For his lost and scattered sheep.
He will never cease his calling,
Until he does safely each one keep.

———————

"For thus saith the Lord God; Behold I, even I,
will both search my sheep, and seek them out."
Ezekiel 34: 11 KJV

C.R. Hill, Jr.

# The Servant's Light

I know of a lighted doorway,
All decked in Christmas greens,
With a pineapple and some apples,
And this is what it means.

The doorway stands for Jesus,
Who came to give us life forevermore.
The apples speak to us of wholeness,
That with his blood he did restore.

The pineapple declares the welcome,
To all who his invitation do believe,
Then daily through their living,
Seek his likeness to receive.

He lived among us as a servant,
He was humble right from the start.
Then taught us that the great among us,
Would have like him a servant's heart.

Now as we again his birth remember,
And seek to see him here among us,
We find him in our servers,
Who in his word do trust.

So thank you for your reminder,
In this world of seekers to be great,
That the greatest ones among us,
Do like Jesus on others wait.

————

"…he that is greatest among you,
let him be as the younger; and he
that is chief, as he that doth serve."
Luke 22: 26 KJV

145

## The Shadow That You Cast

The shadow that you cast today,
Can to another the pathway show;
The Christ who shines in you today,
Will help another to Jesus know.

So mind the shadow today you cast,
Lest to a lesser path it lead,
Keep clean the windows of your soul,
That others see the light of Christ indeed,

No one walks the road of life,
Without a lasting footprint made,
Therefore one must all the more,
Make it a track to others aid.

You never know who on their way,
Will find your lasting mark,
Be sure it leads to the path of light,
Not to everlasting dark.

———————

Read Romans 15: 1 -13

"Let not them that wait on thee, O Lord GOD of hosts,
be ashamed for my sake: let not those that seek thee
be confounded for my sake, O God of Israel."
Psalm 69: 6 KJV

C.R. Hill, Jr.

## The Shepherd's Call

A shepherd sat on a hillside alone,
Sheep were scattered all around,
Yet he hardly noticed all the wolfves,
That stalked and brought them down.

It was as though he didn't care at all,
As long as they left him some to eat.
He wondered why he so empty was,
Why he felt so incomplete.

Then it was God's voice he heard,
And frightening was its sound!
"O shepherd why sit you here,
While my sheep are hunted down?

"Arise! Take up your staff and sling,
Go seek my sheep in danger's claws.
Lead them back into my fold,
And out of death's strong jaws."

---

Read Ezekiel 34: 1-12

"For thus saith the Lord God; Behold, I *even* I,
will both search my sheep, and seek them out.
12 As a shepherd seeketh out his flock in the
day that he is among his sheep *that are* scattered;
so will I seek out my sheep, and will deliver them
out of all places where they have been scattered in
the cloudy and dark day."
Ezekiel 34: 11 & 12 KJV

## The Simple Truth

"It is not a complicated thing,
Although to many it may seem.
All who look on me in faith,
I will their soul redeem.

My Father sent me to the earth,
My life to give for sin,
And for all who put their trust in me,
To raise them up again.

Eternal life I bring to you,
For I have overcome the grave,
And if you will just trust in me,
Your life forever I will save.

There will be trials along your way,
But they are my power to show,
For when others see how you endure,
They will of my power know."

––––––––––

"And Jesus said unto them…40 And this is
the will of him that sent me, that every one
which seeth the Son, and believeth on him,
may have everlasting life: and I will raise
him up at the last day."
John 6:35a & 40 KJV

C.R. Hill, Jr.

## The Thundering Whisper of God

Disheartened is what I had become,
With so many departing from the Lord.
People losing the vision of what they are to be,
That is so clearly made known in God's word.

I thought it no use to give voice to the news,
Having ears it seems none wants to hear.
It's all noise and lights flashing about,
But no message that is really sincere.

Then I was reminded as I looked at God's word,
God leaves himself not with no one to speak,
Even in whispers his words thunder through time,
For the news of his Son will not know defeat.

"Keep spreading the word." He says unto me,
"For as a witness I am not through with you yet.
Though some may seem not hungry to hear,
My message they shall not easily forget."

---

"And the Word was made flesh, and dwelt among us,
(and we beheld his glory, the glory as of the only begotten
of the Father,) full of grace and truth."
John 1: 14 KJV

"God is faithful, by whom ye were called
unto the fellowship of his Son Jesus Christ our Lord"
1Corinthians 1: 9 KJV,

## The Tiny Loaf So Strange

There is a Loaf that offers life,
And feeds the hungry soul.
It satisfies as no other can,
As it makes the wounded whole.

It is not a loaf from a baker's rack,
Nor from earthly flour fine,
But rather it is the bread of God,
Offered to sinful humankind.

Common in appearance yes,
This Loaf of pleasant taste,
Yet it is not an ordinary loaf,
But one of matchless grace.

When we gather in His name,
To share this Loaf so strange,
The life within each tiny bite,
Our broken lives does change.

---

"And as they were eating, Jesus took bread,
and blessed *it*, and brake *it*, and gave *it* to the
disciples, and said, Take, eat; this is my body."
Matthew 26: 26 KJV

C.R. Hill, Jr.

## The Torment of An Unyielding Soul

I like being the boss of me,
I like being the captain of my soul!
I shun surrendering to anyone else,
A single ounce of my control!

That gets in the way of my walk with God,
For I want him to bless what I want to do!
But God won't play life's game my way,
He must be my Lord through and through.

So I struggle with this as most people do,
Who desire to know God as their Lord,
But refuse to yield to his reign over them,
And live fully each day by his Word.

Like Peter of old when asked by the Lord,
"Simon, do you love me more than these?"
Peter couldn't answer straight up that day,
He still wanted himself to please.

This poem cannot end the way that I'd like,
If this battle I do not settle within.
To Jesus I must entirely give up,
Then live daily just following him.

———

Read John 21:15-18

"Verily, verily, I say unto thee, When thou wast young,
thou girdest thyself, and walkedst whither thou wouldest:
but when thou shalt be old, thou shalt stretch forth thy hands,
and another shall gird thee, and carry thee whither thou wouldest not."
John 21: 18 KJV

151

I Talked With Him This Morning

## The Traveler of the Upward Way

Upon the heights a traveler stood,
As he viewed the world below;
Yet no desire in him remained,
To leave the trail and yonder go.

The outside world had lost its allure,
With its hustle, care, and strife.
It was now the challenge of the trail,
That was the passion of his life.

O mountain peaks and steep inclines,
With scarce food and store,
Are not the things the masses crave,
They want ease and things galore.

But to the traveler of the upward way,
Things are but useless weight,
While ease will never build the soul,
Nor lead to Heaven's gate.

———————

"Enter ye in at the strait gate: for wide *is* the gate,
and broad *is* the way, that leadeth to destruction,
and many there be which go in thereat: 14 Because
strait *is* the gate, and narrow *is* the way, which
leadeth unto life, and few there be that find it."
Matthew 7: 13 & 14 KJV

C.R. Hill, Jr.

# The Waiting Vessel

Like an empty vessel beside a stream,
I stand waiting to be filled,
For I like a vessel that by itself,
Can only receive what its Lord has willed.

I cannot tell him in what pool to dip,
Or for what purpose me to use,
To quench his thirst along the way,
Or to share the water of his news.

It may simply be by praising him,
As along the trail we go,
Or in telling others of his love,
So they may of his salvation know.

I can only wait and ready be,
For him to choose the way,
When to fill me, how to use me,
As with him I walk today.

———

"Abide in me, and I in you. As the branch
cannot bear fruit of itself, except it abide in
the vine; no more can ye, except ye abide in me.
15 I am the vine, *ye are* the branches: He that
abideth in me, and I in him, the same bringeth
forth much fruit: for without me ye can do nothing."
John 15: 4-5 KJV

## The Word That Shakes The World

When those first Apostles were told,
To stop preaching in Jesus' name,
They rejoiced in their suffering for him,
And went on preaching just the same.

God was present with mighty works,
To back up the word they brought,
And shook the places where they were,
When him in prayer they sought.

Today many in our world refuse,
What God's faithful ones proclaim,
With covered ears they still cry, "Stop!
Speak to us no more in Jesus' name."

Yet today there are places shaking,
And mighty wonders still taking place,
Wherever believers boldly proclaim,
The news of Jesus' saving grace.

---

"And when they had prayed, the place
was shaken where they were assembled
together; and they were all filled with the
Holy Ghost, and they spake the word of
God with boldness."
Acts 4:31 KJV

C.R. Hill, Jr.

# These

"These" are the problem in most of our lives,
    They were for Peter of old.
"These" are the things between us and God,
    Be they fish, or fame, or gold.

"These" may be the accolades that we seek,
    Like applause or laughs in a show –
A pat on the back, or a hug from a friend,
    The things we all seek as we go.

But whatever are "these" be they fish or fame,
    They are nothing compared to God's grace.
Yet easy it is to get so caught up in "these",
    That they distract us from seeking God's face.

So take stock with me as I examine my life,
    And consider the place "these" do hold.
Have I the will or courage it takes,
Not to let "These" cause me to miss God's goal?

––––––––––

Read John 21: 15 -19

But what things were gain to me, those
I counted loss for Christ. 8 Yea doubtless,
and I count all things *but* loss for the excellency
of the knowledge of Christ Jesus my Lord:
for whom I have suffered the loss of all things,
and do count them *but* dung, that I may win Christ."
Philippians 3:7 & 8 KJV

155

I Talked With Him This Morning

## Thither By Thy Hand I'll Come

When darkness cloaks the trail I walk;
When bad news is all I hear,
Jesus says, "Focus thou on me,
I'll make your pathway clear."

The things we see that cause us fear,
And the unseen things we dread,
Are not a match to cause us harm,
When we trust in what God said.

So I'll walk this path I am on,
Though fog and darkness obscure,
Trusting in God's guiding hand,
For he makes each step secure.

And when at last I reach my goal,
When in triumph I the lowlands scan,
I'll lift my voice in eternal praise,
Having arrived by God's kind hand.

———————

"Surely he shall not be moved for ever:
the righteous shall be in  everlasting
remembrance. 7 He shall not be afraid
of evil tidings: his heart is fixed, trusting
in the LORD. 8 His heart *is* established, he
shall not be afraid, until he see *his desire*
upon his enemies."
Psalm 112: 6 – 8 KJV

C.R. Hill, Jr.

## Thy Kingdom Come

I heard a word from God today,
Of his great salvation's love.
How his desire for all his flock,
To live on earth as they live above.

To dwell in safety with naught to fear,
From neither beast nor fellow man,
And eat the fruits of his good earth,
Given by his kind abundant hand.

O to see his desire come true,
Instead of the killings that we see.
In place of all the fear and hate,
O Lord, let your kingdom come to be.

Here on earth as there in heaven,
May your name be hallowed by each one,
And may your Word be reverenced now,
As all the earth turns to your Son.

———————

"And they shall no more be a prey to the
heathen, neither shall the beast of the
land devour them; but they shall dwell
safely, and none shall make *them* afraid."
Ezekiel 34: 28 KJV

## To A Faithful Witness Be

I saw a glimpse of God today,
I saw that a tear was in his eye,
I wondered what it was that hurt him so,
Then I saw it was the sins of you and I.

Forgive me LORD for the things I've done,
For every unclean thought and deed.
Forgive me for the hurt I've caused,
And for ignoring those in need.

O teach me Father thy path to choose,
To walk in the way that Jesus made.
Help me to share with all I meet,
The price that for their life you paid.

Then when my journey here is done,
When they lay me down to rest,
May it be said in heaven above,
He passed in life the faithful test.

———————

"Behold, the eye of the LORD *is* upon
them that fear him, upon them that hope
in his mercy; 19 To deliver their soul from
death, and to keep them alive in famine."
Psalm 33: 18 &19 KJV

## To Be Fishers of Men

Peter was called along with his brothers,
To leave their old fishing hole.
"Get out of your boat and come follow me.
For you to be fishing for men is God's goal."

Peter obeyed and followed that day,
Though to do so was for him a big stretch.
For according to Luke that call came the day,*
That he had made a boat-sinking catch.

It happened again after Jesus had risen,
On a morning when Peter went back to the sea.
After catching more fish than they could haul in,
Jesus said, "Now Peter, you come follow me."**

It is nothing to hear and answer God's call,
When the chips are down and you're all out of hope.
But in the good times when Jesus says, "come,"
Can you like Jesus, say to the devil, "Nope!"?***

———————

Read Matthew 4: 1- 25

*Luke 5: 1- 22
**John 21: 1 -22
***Matthew 4: 8 – 10

"And he saith unto them, Follow me, and
I will make you fishers of men.."
Matthew 4:19 KJV

I Talked With Him This Morning

## To Have the Mind of Jesus

I've been chasing a dream of my own,
For as long as I can remember.
Even when doing God's work I thought,
It was to my own glory I hoped it to render.

How easy it is to fall into this trap,
And do good in hopes of our gain,
We say it is God's work we're tending to,
But we hope to enhance our own name.

How different is what Jesus has taught,
By the example he set with his life.
He went to the cross to save you and me,
Disregarding its pain and its strife.

He calls us to follow and do as he did,
When the needs of others we face.
We're to forget our own self interest;
As we offer through Jesus, God's grace.

----------

"Look not every man on his own things,
but every man also on the things of others.
5 Let this mind be in you which was also
in Christ Jesus."
Philippians 2:4 & 5KJV

In the Greek the "also" of verse 4
does not occur rendering the verse:

*Look not every man on his own things,*
*but every man on the things of others..*

To get the full meaning of this 4<sup>th</sup> verse
read it from one of the more recent translations
leaving out the **only** and the **also**.

C.R. Hill, Jr.

# To Know the Name of God

If junk food is all my body craves,
Good taste that does not nourish,
How then could I ever expect,
In perfect health my life to flourish?

Can it with my soul be different?
If I only chose what the world prescribes,
How can ever I expect to become,
One in whom God's Son abides?

The name of God does nourish the soul,
When he in an intimate walk is known.
It is the heart where God's name abides,
When Jesus makes that soul his own.

Oh may I hunger for his word each day,
May I thirst to his name fully know,
Then may his love in me abide,
And thus always to others show.

---

Read John 17

"And I have declared unto them thy name,
and will declare *it*: that the love wherewith
thou hast loved me may be in them, and I in them."
John 17:26 KJV

161

I Talked With Him This Morning

## To Run With The Horsemen

Upward go fly with the eagles,
With the horsemen go swiftly to run.
Go capture the flag in life's contest,
Relying for strength on God's Son.

Though others may never get airborne,
For wearied by footmen they've been,
You will soar the heavens like eagles,
Riding God's Spirit like wind.

The horsemen will raise up their challenge,
Mounted on steeds sleek and swift,
But you will compete without tiring,
With the Spirit of God as your gift.

Exhausted and spent they will stumble,
Though youthful and strong they appear,
While you will be strolling triumphant,
When to relying on God you adhere.

---------

"Even the youths shall faint and be weary,
and the young men shall utterly fall: 31 But
they that wait upon the LORD shall renew
*their* strength; they shall mount up with wings
as eagles; they shall run, and not be weary;
*and* they shall walk, and not faint."
Isaiah 40: 30 & 31 KJV

C.R. Hill, Jr.

# Treasures in the Trash

It was junk – just assorted parts,
Pilled on my old scrap heap.
Nothing there I thought at first,
That I would want to keep.

But then I took a closer look,
And saw a treasure in that trash.
Something unique could come of it,
If I would invest some time and cash.

So many times we've seen a life,
On some scrap heap thrown.
We thought not worth the time of day,
Yet if we had to God their value known.

For God sees things beyond our view,
Like treasures hidden in a field.
Thus he invests his love through Christ,
And to us a treasure is revealed.

––––––––––

"But we have this treasure in earthen vessels,
that the excellency of the power may be of God,
and not of us."
2Corinthians 4: 7 KJV

163

## Triumph in the Tempest

There are often storms that arise on our sea,
And they threaten our lives to undo.
But when it is with Jesus you sail,
The storms are to further his plans for you.

So the next time the winds and waves get up,
And you feel your life being swamped,
Focus not on the waves, but Jesus' face,
Then experience your faith being prompted.

Jesus does not call us to lives full of ease,
For lives left unchallenged grow weak,
The storms are occasions to strengthen our faith,
For in them his presence we seek.

So welcome the storms that arise on your sea,
As occasions to grow closer to God.
The winds and the waves are not greater than he,
And to sleep peaceful when they rage is not odd.

———

Read Matthew 8:18-27

"And he saith unto them, Why are ye fearful,
O ye of little faith? Then he arose, and rebuked
the winds and the sea; and there was a great calm.
Matthew 8: 26 KJV

C.R. Hill, Jr.

## Victory Stars

The poor oppressed and trampled down,
Deprived of joy, and friends with pain,
Have in the light of heaven's news,
But to look to Jesus and victory gain.

No one wants to share the lot,
Of the mournful, poor, and meek.
So we strive through power and pride,
To avoid such plight, and blessing seek.

Some folks lie at the Sheep Gate pool,*
Blaming others for their desperate plight,
But some see Jesus, and their spirit stirs,
Then rise as victors by heaven's light.

So come to Jesus – let his power bless,
All your wounds and victim scars,
For by the grace that his love provides,
These can become your victory stars.

––––––––––

Read John 5: 2-9

"When Jesus saw him lie, and knew that
he had been now a long time in that case,
he saith unto him, Wilt thou be made whole?"
John 5:6 KJV

165

## Walking Patches

Breathe deep and slow,
The air is thin up here,
Not like down below.
Up here the soul can breathe,
The heart can learn to hear,
And even on a dreary day,
The mind can see things clear.

Look! Beside the leafy trail,
Patches on the point,
Has he caught the scent of quail?
More likely grouse.
Steady boy, let me make the flush.
Ah ha grouse!
Have you ever heard such Fuss?

Sorry boy.
You know I don't have a gun,
We're just out to walk,
And have this little fun.

## C.R. Hill, Jr.

Listen, it's still again,
Save for the ghostly flight of falling leaves,
And the whisper of the wind.
Come boy, it's getting dark.
Best we be getting home,
All Hallows Eve is not the time,
For us to be in these woods alone.

What? You say I fell asleep.
It was the lullaby of falling rain,
And the drug of fireplace heat.
I talked? You heard me mention grouse.
I was walking Patches,
Though I never left the house.

Up here the soul can breathe,
And the heart can learn to hear,
Even dreaming by the fireplace,
The mind can see things clear.

———

"Be still and know that I *am* God:"
Psalm 46: 10 KJV

## Walking By Faith

The way ahead though veiled in fog,
Lies before me for the taking,
And in trust I must go forth,
Assured God the road is making.

He said to Abram, "Go out from here,
To a land that I will show you."
And Abram went not knowing where,
Until God's promise did come true.

Down through the ages men of faith,
Have ventured into the vast unknown,
Just trusting in the word of God,
To lead them to a better home.

So now to you and me it comes,
In these uncertain days,
To likewise walk in faith with God,
And follow in his righteous ways.

———————

"Now the LORD had said unto Abram,
Get thee out of thy country, and from
thy kindred, and from thy father's house,
unto a land that I will shew thee; 2 And I
will make of thee a great nation, and I will
bless thee, and make thy name great;
and thou shalt be a blessing:"
Genesis 12: 1 & 2 KJV

C.R. Hill, Jr.

# Water from the Rock

Out of the heart of one who believes,
Shall the living waters flow,
Yet it is from God's rock the water springs,
This from God's word we know.

Thus how can water flow out of one's heart,
Unless it by God's spring is fed?
That is one must have the rock in one's heart,
Not just know about Jesus in their head.

Living water that flows out of one's life,
Is the overflow of an abundance inside,
There is a pool where Jesus resides,
That flows out in a joyful tide.

So be thirsty my children, long for the Lord,
Then in faith invite Jesus to come in.
Your heart will be filled until it overflows,
And you will never be thirsty again.

―――――――

"O GOD, thou *art* my God; early will
I seek thee: my soul thirsteth for thee,
my flesh longeth for thee in a dry and
thirsty land, where no water is;"
Psalm 63: 1 KJV

"In the last day, that great *day* of the feast,
Jesus stood and cried, saying, If any man thirst,
let him come unto me, and drink. 38 He that
believeth on me, as the scripture hath said,
out of his belly shall flow rivers of living water."
John 7: 37b & 38 KJV

## We Live!

Is there anything on earth,
That can have it any louder said,
Than a valley full of old dried bones,
To say, "These folks are really dead!"?

O Ezekiel saw the wheel way up in the sky,
Amazing that it was, yet nothing like as real,
As is the vision of those old dried bones,
When faced by death the way we feel.

In our eyes death appears so final.
Powerless we are to turn away its tide!
When death's icy hand snuffs away one's life,
No power of earth can change the fact they died.

So what is this unseen hope in Christ,
That we Christians hold so tight?
It is trusting him who did Jesus raise,
Will also deliver us from death's dark night.

———

Read Ezekiel 37: 1-14 & Romans 8: 6 - 11

"And he said unto me, Son of man,
can these bones live: And I answered,
O Lord GOD, thou knowest. 4 And he
said unto me, Prophesy upon these bones,
and say unto them, O ye dry bones,
hear the word of the LORD."
Ezekiel 37: 3 & 4 KJV

"But if the Spirit of him that raised up
Jesus from the dead dwell in you, he that
raised up Christ from the dead shall also
quicken your mortal bodies by his Spirit
that dwelleth in you."
Romans 8: 11 KJV

170

C.R. Hill, Jr.

# What Do You Think?

What is it you are thinking friend,
What thoughts fill your mind?
Out of the abundance of the heart,
Your words and deeds expression find.

Let passion or a sinful lust,
Fill your heart with deep desire;
Covet things that you don't have,
Or let anger fill your heart with fire.

These are the kind of thoughts,
That will quickly lead your life astray,
But lift your thoughts unto God's hills,
And you will walk in praise each day.

Jesus gives you his Holy Spirit,
So you may live the way you ought,
Let your thoughts be on God's word,
And your life express the things he taught.

————

"I will lift up mine eyes unto the hills,
from whence cometh my help. 2 My help
*cometh* from the LORD, which made
heaven and earth."
Psalm 121: 1 & 2 KJV

"I will sing unto the LORD as long as I live:
I will sing praise to my God while I have my
being. 34 My meditation of him shall be sweet:
I will be glad in the LORD."
Psalm 104: 33 & 34 KJV

I Talked With Him This Morning

## What We Need Now

Here is the thing we need today;
That our hearts be rent,
So we will awaken from sin's sleep,
And of our godlessness repent.

Sin has drugged our world until,
We have lost all sense of wrong,
Whatever evil comes into vogue,
We just blindly go along.

Who is there among us to cry,
"The Emperor has no clothes!"
And open us to see the shame,
Of this path to death we chose?

May we hear God's word anew,
Let it our hearts now open wide,
To receive the truth it has for us,
That it is for our sins that Jesus died.

———

"Now when they heard *this*, they were pricked
in their heart, and said unto Peter and to the rest
of the apostles, Men *and* brethren, what shall we do?
38 Then Peter said unto them, Repent, and be baptized
every one of you in the name of Jesus Christ for the
remission of sins, and ye shall receive the gift of the
Holy Ghost. 39 For the promise is unto you, and to
your children, and to all that are afar off, *even* as
many as the Lord our God shall call."
Acts 2: 37 – 39 KJV

C.R. Hill, Jr.

# When Come the Unfair Tides

Some times the tides of life,
Take for us such an unfair turn,
That we want to cry out in rage,
Then we must from Jesus learn.

None was more unfairly treated,
Than was Jesus at his trial;
Yet he said not a single word,
As he was tortured all the while.

Oh he could have in anguish cried,
Even turned the tides around.
But instead he bore it all for us,
So we could now be righteous found.

When from the cross he looked on those,
Who the nails had driven in,
He asked God to forgive them all,
For what they had done to him.

————

"He was oppressed, and he was afflicted,
yet he opened not his mouth: he is brought
as a lamb to the slaughter, and as a sheep
before her shearers is dumb, so he openeth
not his mouth."
Isaiah 53: 7 KJV

I Talked With Him This Morning

## When Jesus Is The Helmsman

Give all you've got to living by faith,
Holding nothing back in reserve,
Then stand back and get out of the way,
Letting God your living preserve.

Circumstances of time can look very dim,
And conditions can faith overwhelm,
Until you commit to trusting God anyway,
Putting Jesus himself at the helm.

When the Master of time, and eternity too,
Pilots your life's ship,
There is not a storm that can overcome you,
Regardless how relentless its grips.

So take heart O child whatever life brings,
For your life is safe in God's hands,
Time's wind and her waves always will yield,
Whenever God's Son gives commands.

———————

"And they feared exceedingly, and said
one to another, What manner of man is this,
that even the wind and the sea obey him."
Mark 4:41 KJV

C.R. Hill, Jr.

## When The Final Whistle Blows

So much of what we see today,
Is evil, dark, and mean.
How are folks to believe God reigns,
When the evening news they've seen?

It seems the world has lost its way,
Who today knows right from wrong?
Most appear to think it matters not,
So with whatever they go along.

Do any realize that God is watching?
He patiently bides his time.
In hope, it must be, he is waiting,
For one more soul their way to find.

But when evil has reached full bloom,
When it looks like Satan will have his way,
Then for the sake of his faithful ones,
God will step in with Judgment Day.

————

Read Psalm 68: 1-10 & Matthew 24: 1-22

"Let God arise, let his enemies be scattered:
let them also that hate him flee before him.
2 As smoke is driven away, *so* drive *them* away:
as wax melteth before the fire, so let the wicked
perish at the presence of God."
Psalm 68: 1& 2 KJV,

"And Jesus answered…And except those
days should be shortened, there should no
flesh be saved: but for the elect's sake
those days shall be shortened."
Matthew 24: 4a & 22 KJV

175

I Talked With Him This Morning

## Where O Nation Do You Now Stand?

The Bible says that they are blessed,
Who in God their trust do put,
The nation that makes the Lord their God,
Will not be trodden under an invader's foot.

Yet when a people who once were faithful,
From the righteous way have turned,
The wrath of God they then incur,
With the reward their deeds have earned.

It is not enough to once have loved
God's word and done his will,
It daily takes a faithful land,
If God is to their freedom's dream fulfill.

Look now o land of brave and free,
How has your walk become?
Do you in truth still honor God,
Or live faithful to God's Son?

---

"Let all the earth fear the LORD: let all the inhabitants
of the world stand in awe of him 9 For he spake, and
it was *done*; he commanded, and it stood fast.
10 The LORD bringeth the counsel of the heathen to nought:
he maketh the devices of the people of none effect.
11 The counsel of the LORD standeth for ever, the thoughts
of his heart to all generations. 12 Blessed *is* the nation whose
God is the LORD; *and* the people *whom* he hath chosen for his
own inheritance."
Psalm 33: 8 – 12 KJV

C.R. Hill, Jr.

## Where The Heart Is Focused

When we shall make the Lord our God,
And walk faithful in his ways,
He will in turn bless our land,
And make us prosper all our days.

But when we turn our hearts away;
When we for ourselves do idols make,
Then God turns his back on us,
And we suffer for our mistake.

Look around and give some thought,
How many idols do you have?
They may not be of wood or stone,
Or look like some golden calf.

But idols and the things we place,
Before the honoring of God's name.
We may not bow before a statue,
But things we worship just the same.

———————

Read Leviticus 26: 1 - 13

"Ye shall make you no idols nor graven image,
neither rear you up a standing image, neither
shall ye set up *any* image of stone in your land,
to bow down unto it: for I *am* the LORD your God."
Leviticus 26: 1 KJV

"If my people, which are called by my name,
shall humble themselves, and pray, and seek
my face, and turn from their wicked ways; then
will I hear from heaven, and will forgive their sin,
and will heal their land."
2Chronicles 7: 14 KJV

## White Blazes

I sought the path of yonder narrow gate,
I've chosen to make it my way,
Yet I have discovered as there I climb,
There are side trails that would lead me astray.

"Blue blazes" they're called by hikers who know.
They are the shortcuts around the hard climbs.
Detours that take one off the main trail,
Away from traveling the path God designs.

I find these trails tempting to take,
They are easier and with company to share,
Yet I know if I take them instead of my path,
That goal that I seek – I'll never get there!

So I will resolve at the start of each day,
As a purist to hike, taking every white blaze,*
Studying closely the guide God has provided,
And the pattern I find in Christ's ways.

———

"Hold fast the form of sound words,
which thou hast heard of me, in faith
and love which is in Christ Jesus."
2Timothy 1:13 KJV

*The Appalachian Trail is marked by
"white blazes" while other secondary trails
along its way are marked by "blue blazes."

C.R. Hill, Jr.

# Whole Hearted Desire

I've stood guard through the morning watch,
And longed for the coming dawn.
I've seen the monsters shadows make,
And longed for the night to be gone.

So I know what the Psalmist is saying,
When he longs for the Lord to appear.
One has to want him with all of their heart,
If they are to walk with him here.

There is no halfway to be a follower of Christ;
No partial commitment will suffice.
The mission he's on requires all that one has,
Nor can one think about following twice.

He invites us to follow, and his company keep,
He desires that we travel with him,
For he has a great task to accomplish here,
And millions of lost souls here to win.

———————

"My soul waiteth for the Lord more than
they that watch for the morning: *I say, more
than* they that watch for the morning."
Psalm 130: 6 KJV

"And Jesus said unto him, No man, having
put his hand to the plough, and looking back,
is fit for the kingdom of God."
Luke 9:62 KJV

I Talked With Him This Morning

## Will You Be At The Wedding?

Some of you must work today,
And will not be in a church pew sitting;
Yet while you go about your jobs,
Do not be your Lord forgetting.

Some of you are at play today,
Enjoying your weekend pleasure,
Still as you go on having fun,
Don't overlook life's greatest treasure.

God has sent to earth his Son,
To redeem his church forever,
Through death he paid for all her sins,
So they may be held against her never.

By his resurrection from the grave,
He won for her eternal life,
And he will be coming back some day,
To take her to heaven as his wife.

———————

"And I saw a new heaven and a new earth:
for the first heaven and the first earth were
passed away; and there was no more sea.
2 And I John saw the holy city, new Jerusalem,
coming down from God out of heaven, prepared
as a bride adorned for her husband."
Revelation 21: 1& 2 KJV

C.R. Hill, Jr.

# With Reverence and Awe

It seems the church is losing ground,
In many quarters of our land.
Perhaps we Christians share the blame,
For not taking a clearer stand.

Far too casual we have become,
In our worship of our Lord.
We like the "feel good" gospel news,
But avoid the judgment in God's word.

God is a God of grace that's true,
In Jesus Christ he shows us his love.
To save the world is his great desire,
And reconcile earth to heaven above.

To himself the world to reconcile,
God does not to sin and evil condescend.
He calls us each one to repent and trust,
If we hope to forever live with him.

———————

"But ye are come unto mount Zion, and unto
the city of the living God, the heavenly Jerusalem,
and to an innumerable company of angels, 23 To the
general assembly and church of the firstborn, which
are written in heaven, and to God the Judge of all, and
to the spirits of just men made perfect, 24 And to Jesus
the mediator of the new covenant, and to the blood of
sprinkling, that speaketh better things than *that of* Abel...
28 Wherefore we receiving a kingdom which cannot be
moved, let us have grace, whereby we may serve God
acceptably with reverence and godly fear: 29 For our God
*is* a consuming fire."
Hebrews 12: 22 -24 & 28 – 29 KJV

## Yet Comes the King of Glory

Jesus is forever the Almighty,
Who is and was and is to come.
Jesus is the King of glory,
He is God's Only Son.

Yet how hard for us to listen,
With so many centuries now gone by?
We see Christmas decorations,
But the Christ Child we deny.

Still the birth stories we enjoy,
And the carols we do still sing,
But we lack the true conviction,
Of the message that they bring.

Awake O sleeping people,
Arise you slumbering souls!
The King of glory is among us,
In our midst his presence strolls.

He was, he is, and is to come,
And every knee shall bow,
Then every tongue shall thunder,
"O Lord have mercy on us now!"

———————

[Jesus] "Who is the image of the invisible God, the firstborn of every creature: 16 For by him were all things created, that are in heaven, and that are in earth, visible and invisible, whether *they be* thrones, or dominions, or principalities, or powers: all things were created by him and for him: 17 And he is before all things, and by him all things consist. 18 And he is the head of the body, the church: who is the beginning, the firstborn from the dead; that in all *things* he might have the preeminence. 19 For it pleased *the Father* that in him should all fulness dwell; 20 And, having made peace through the blood of his cross, by him to reconcile all things unto himself; by him, I say, whether *they be* things in earth, or in heaven."
Colossians 1: 15 – 20 KJV

C.R. Hill, Jr.

# Yet Shall I Praise Him

It matters not who the enemy is,
Whether nation, or thief, or disease,
Their power is always neutralized,
When to God we go on our knees.

Our soul can be deeply troubled within,
Our future can look very dark.
Until we return to God's holy hill,
And find shelter in the depths of his ark.

O look up my soul,
Do not thou despair!
Even in the darkness of midnight,
God's presence resides with you there.

Lift up your voice in glorious praise,
Sing with the joy of God's love!
Salvation lies not with the kingdoms of men,
It resides with Jesus above.

---

"Why art thou cast down, O my soul?
And why art thou disquieted within me?
Hope in God: for I shall yet praise him,
*who is* the health of my countenance,
and my God."
Psalm 43: 5 KJV

I Talked With Him This Morning

## You Can Be More Than You Are

Why descend to life's baser things,
For the style of life you choose?
Jesus has shown you the perfect way,
Why not aspire to fill his shoes?

So many whom we see these days,
Seem to have no self-esteem;
Yet Jesus values them worth his life,
That they may aspire to living his dream.

Now you my friend the choice have,
Of the person you will become,
Follow others on the downward path,
Or aspire to live like God's Son.

Old Simon was of that baser sort,
Until Jesus that day he met.
He received a name from God above,
Now Saint Peter who can forget?

---

"...*ye are* a chosen generation, a royal priesthood,
an holy nation, a peculiar people; that ye should shew
forth the praises of him who hath called you out of
darkness into his marvellous light; 10 Which in time past
*were* not a people, but *are* now the people of God:
which had not obtained mercy, but now have obtained mercy."
1Peter 2: 9 & 10 KJV

"As obedient children, not fashioning yourselves
according to the former lusts in your ignorance.
15 But as he which hath called you is holy, so be
ye holy in all manner of conversation; 16 Because
it is written, BE YE HOLY; FOR I AM HOLY."
1Peter 1: 14-16 KJV

C.R. Hill, Jr.

## Your Heart A Home For God

Like a lonesome nomad,
God throughout the earth does roam,
He is searching for a dwelling,
A heart where he can make his home.

He is looking not for a rich man,
Or a woman of fleshly beauty,
Not a person with special talents,
Or someone obsessed with duty.

The heart that God is seeking,
Is the one fully trusting in his Son,
Into such hearts with Jesus,
He comes to live with them as one.

Today when you hear him knocking,
Open your heart wide,
Invite him in to spend each moment,
And throughout your life abide.

---

"Jesus answered and said unto him,
If a man love me, he will keep my words:
and my Father will love him, and we will
come unto him, and make our abode with him."
John 14:23 KJV

Dr. C. R. Hill, Jr. is an ordained United Methodist Minister in the North Georgia Conference of the United Methodist Church. He began his ministry following his tour of duty in the U.S. Army. C. R. has an AA degree from Emmanuel College in Franklin Springs, Georgia, and a BSED from the University of Georgia in Athens, Georgia. He received his MDIV and DMIN degrees from Emory University's Candler School of Theology in Atlanta, Georgia. He has served under appointment in pastoral ministry since 1963 having served twelve congregations. Among them Peachtree Road UMC in Atlanta and Conyers First UMC in Conyers, Georgia. As Senior Pastor of McDonough First UMC for thirteen years where he led that congregation to grow in membership by 100% and establish the Wesley Way United Methodist Church. Likewise at Canton First UMC for ten years the congregation grew by 100% and built a 900 seat worship and educational complex.

In addition to his pastoral ministry C. R. has served on numerous conference and district boards and agencies. Included among these the Board of Ordained Ministries for eight years, and the Conference Committee on Global Ministries for eight years. He served as Chair of the Griffin District Committee on Ordained Ministries for eight years. He has also served as Dean of the North Georgia School of Christian Missions. From 2001 to 2011, and from 2014 to the present he has served on the Reinhardt University Board of Trustees. C. R. has written hundreds of sermons, poems, and articles as well as published three previous books, *Between Two Worlds*, *Light From Beyond the Veil*, and *Through The Frosted Window*.

C. R. retired at the 2011 session of the North Georgia Conference. He now continues in ministry through serving as a Hospital Chaplain, and writing. When he is not busy with these endeavors he enjoys bicycling, along with reconditioning and restoring vintage bicycles, woodcarving, reading, and fly fishing.

C. R and his wife Jackie celebrated their fifty-second year of marriage in November of 2014. They have two married children, three grandsons, and one granddaughter-in-law.

CPSIA information can be obtained
at www.ICGtesting.com
Printed in the USA
LVOW13s2338280617

539740LV00006B/316/P

9 781940 395913